ENDORSEMENTS

As many Asian American churches encounter a growing number of continuing and new challenges, this "letter" aims to provide a fresh infusion of hope and direction by reminding them of their unique calling "for such a time as this." Written by Asian American Christian leaders who are practitioners first, these stories of faithful resilience, contextualized ministry practices, and faith-filled dreams will inspire readers by enabling them to see what God is doing in and through a wide range of Asian American churches today.

Peter Cha, Professor of Church, Culture, and Society, Trinity Evangelical Divinity School

It's important to hear the voices and perspectives of those who serve on the margins of what is often considered mainstream in the United States. This includes hearing from Asian American pastors and ministry leaders. In this compilation of reflections, essays, and thoughtfully written chapters, the reader gains a glimpse into a segment of the beautiful mosaic of the Asian American church. You will mine treasures from the depth of their experiences as ministry leaders, which also reflects the experiences of many others from an East Asian Christian background. Asian American Christians have a substantial gift that the whole church can be blessed with—and this book wonderfully displays that reality.

Raymond Chang, President of Asian American Christian Collaborative/ Executive Director of TENx10

For many years, churches in the US were told they should all aim to become multiethnic churches. Although churches should never segregate, Asian American churches were made to think they were less biblical and less pleasing to the Lord because of its specialization.

So, I was delighted to read this book that affirms and celebrates the Asian American church. It takes a variety of different types of churches to reach the world with the gospel. The Asian American church, where Asian Americans can feel at home and grow spiritually with those with similar cultural experiences, should be valued for its unique strengths. This book provides much needed encouragement and sound advice for the next generation of Asian American church leaders.

Steven Chin, Senior Pastor Emeritus, Boston Chinese Evangelical Church

With such a shortage of published resources, this book is a gift to the Asian American church. The authors are seasoned practitioners who love the local church. Their reflections offer sound principles for effective ministry and leadership formation in any ministry setting. I intend to make it required reading for my practical ministry courses.

Dr. Daniel K. Eng, faculty member at Western Seminary and Governing Board member, Portland Chinese C&MA Church

The challenges of Asian American ministry are not unfamiliar to those who have been serving in the trenches. Yet the exciting opportunities are limitless with the Lord's direction and power. In this blessing of a book, Steve Chang and an ensemble of experienced Asian American Christian leaders provide a realistic but hopeful perspective on Asian American ministry's past, present, and future. What is the purpose of the Asian American church? Read and see how God works and will continue to work for his glory.

Matthew D. Kim, Professor of Practical Theology and Raborn Chair of Pastoral Leadership, Baylor University's Truett Seminary, Coauthor of *Finding Our Voice: A Vision for Asian North American Preaching*

In this timely "Letter," wise and faithful Asian American church leaders have provided us with much clarity and compassion as we strive to serve God and others in our unique cultural time, space, and history. Though written primarily about, for, and to the Asian American Christian church, this is a resource that can be a rich blessing for anyone seeking to honor Christ and his kingdom. Read it and be blessed, so you can be a blessing to others.

Rev. Julius J. Kim, PhD, Teaching Pastor & Consultant, Onnuri Church Visiting Professor, Westminster Seminary California

A Letter to the Asian American Church is a timely exploration of identity, spirituality, and community. Through insightful theological reflections and compelling testimonies, this collection sympathetically addresses the challenges of racialization among Asian American Christians.

Past studies of European immigrant religions have posited a generational decline of ethnic affiliation as the children of immigrants follow the assimilationist path. However, for Asian Americans, ethnic culture and racialization continue to impact their sense of belonging and acceptance in mainstream churches. Asian American churches serve as creative communities of belonging and resolution to the constraints and opportunities tied to multiple identities.

This engaging work is an important resource and contribution to the emerging literature on Asian American Christianity.

> **Sharon Kim**, Professor of Sociology, California State University Fullerton. Author of *A Faith of Our Own*

"Better Together." That's the phrase that resounds in my heart after reading this book. "Better Together." God demonstrates that with us! He can do a much better job by himself, but he calls us to work with him! As a pastor working in the first-generation Korean immigrant church context, I am so thankful that we can work side by side as brothers and sisters in Christ. I am grateful for our partnership in the gospel. Together, I believe we can better lay the groundwork for God's kingdom for the next generation. I am also thankful for this book, and I hope and pray that God will use many insights and experiences of Asian churches to build his kingdom through broken people like us! Great job, partners. We are better together!

> **Rev. Tae Kim**, Senior Pastor of ANC Onnuri Church in Sunland, CA

As I was reading *A Letter to the Asian American Church*, a few distinct feelings arose. First, I felt heard and embraced as a fellow Asian American ministry practitioner. The authors, while writing from their unique context and stories, all spoke to me directly. As a long time, church ministry veteran, I felt like my story was being spoken and my voice being heard. I felt like I was being loved and cared for. I felt like my story was being affirmed and embraced. Second, I felt tears of empathy and hope. The stories of each ministry practitioner were stories I could feel deeply and relate to. Their pain, struggles, and perhaps most of all, hope, was expressed in ways that were directly touching and relevant to me. Third and finally, I felt equipped and encouraged. Whether directly relevant to my own ministry context or not, I felt the practical ministry applications of the authors/practitioners were deeply helpful and useful to fellow present and emerging Asian American leaders. Overall, this book will serve as a shining light of hope and learning for those who read it.

Danny Kwon, PhD, Senior Director of Youth Ministry Content and Cross-Cultural Initiatives at Rooted Ministries, Adjunct Professor of Christian Leadership

Moving beyond the popular but flawed multiethnic church propaganda with its generic discipleship, hidden syncretism, and shallow justice, these brave Asian American pastors affirm the call and place of the Asian immigrant church and the Asian American church. While all of us must move toward the vision of the Kingdom, these churches have a critical role in God's mixed economy ecclesiology. No apology for their existence is necessary. Through their pastoral reflections, they address the problem of narrative scarcity in Asian American ministry resources by moving us one step toward narrative plenitude with diverse stories and perspectives. Hopefully, more will join them, continually sharpening how to do ministry and to articulate ourselves theologically as Asian Americans, improving with each iteration.

Daniel D. Lee, Academic Dean of the Center for Asian American Theology and Ministry at Fuller Theological Seminary and author of *Doing Asian American Theology*

I was saved through the ministry of the Asian immigrant church in my late teenage years and have been a beneficiary of the Asian American church ever since. It is a gift to have this collection of essays written by ministry leaders who have faithfully labored in these contexts. With their unique perspectives and experiences, they together remind us of the unique dignity of the Asian immigrant and Asian American church. They provide us with hard-earned wisdom to guide us through the particular complexities and opportunities before us. They help deepen our conviction that this ministry matters—to the people around us now and to the future generations to come, and to God. Each of us have a unique and precious calling to steward. I feel encouraged, better equipped, and deeply hopeful at all that God can and will accomplish in and through our Asian American faith community as we seek to advance his kingdom together.

Esther Liu, CCEF Faculty Member & Counselor, Author of *Shame: Being Known & Loved*

I'm excited about this book. I'm excited because this is who I am. This is my community. This is my family. This is my experience. I personally want to be a part of the HOPE and the FUTURE that this book is all about. And I hope you do as well. If you are Asian American, I think you will find so many points of heart and head resonance. And if you are not, I trust that there is so much for you to learn as well. Because whether or not you are Asian American, the road ahead will be an exciting challenge, and we have the opportunity to journey down it together as the body of Christ in our uniqueness and in our unity.

Michael Young-Suk Oh, CEO, Lausanne Movement

At a time when the American church seems to be on life support and has seemingly lost its mission, vision, and direction, there are signs of life that God has graciously prepared and revealed. Drawing from the breadth and depth of the Asian American Christian community curated by the SOLA Network, this text brings insight and inspiration for the revival and renewal of the church. A future hope for the American church can be found within this text and the American Church would do well to receive these prophetic and pastoral words from the Asian American Christian community.

Soong-Chan Rah, Robert Munger Professor of Evangelism, Fuller Theological Seminary and Author of *The Next Evangelicalism* and *Prophetic Lament*

Congratulations to the contributors of *A Letter to the Asian American Church*! This book brings a fresh perspective to an ongoing discussion related to the challenges and celebrations of life in the Asian American church. A strength of this work is the wide range of authors, including younger, older, male, female, vocational pastors, and lay leaders, giving a comprehensive voice to the multiple issues that face the Asian American church. This work is a must for the lay person, the seminarian, deacon, elder, or the veteran pastor/leader who wants to understand the different layers of the Asian American church.

Benjamin C. Shin, Associate Professor of Christian Ministry & Leadership at Talbot School of Theology

I am an immigrant pastor who believes that the future of the Asian American church rests in the second generation—the generation who grows up in the US, embraces the culture of the land, identifies with the happenings around them, and remains where they are in order to be a part of the solutions to the complex issues that afflict this land.

This book is a part of the movement that attempts to earn the trust of the first generation while empowering the second generation to stand up to the challenge. I heartily endorse the voices represented in this book.

Make no mistake, bridging the diversity within the Asian American church is a high calling but hard work, a lot of hard work. But it is worthy of our every effort to contribute to the building up of the Asian American church because that's who we are in Christ.

Pastor Albert Ting, Senior Pastor of First Chinese Baptist Church Walnut and Former President of Singapore Bible College

I was impressed at how the chapter authors of *A Letter to the Asian American Church* wove together Scripture and their personal and church experiences. To the credit of the editor, Steve S. Chang, those experiences arose from numerous regions in the United States. I like how pertinent themes such as navigating contextualization and the honor–shame culture permeate the work. As a result of going through the book, my interest in and praying for the Asian American church grew. This book will prove influential for years to come!

Daniel L. Wong, coauthor of *Finding Our Voice: A Vision for Asian American Preaching*, retired Associate Professor of Christian Ministries, Tyndale University.

A Letter to the
Asian American Church
Embracing the Call

Edited by Steve S. Chang

A Letter to the Asian American Church: Embracing the Call
Categories: Christian Books & Bibles | Churches & Church Leadership

Copyright 2024 SOLA Network

Brea, California, USA
SOLA.NETWORK

ISBN 9798875726330

Publishing Manager: Aaron Lee
Cover, Design, and Typesetting: Jessica Lee

ACKNOWLEDGMENTS

We are grateful to everyone connected to SOLA Network—the council, staff, editorial board, and conference team. Your commitment to influencing the emerging generation of Asian Americans with the gospel of Jesus Christ is precisely what we need in this crucial time. Thank you so much for giving of your time, gifts, and faithfulness.

We are also grateful for individuals and churches who have invested in the work of SOLA on so many levels. Thank you for enabling us to serve the broader church community.

We also acknowledge and appreciate those who have contributed to this project including Aaron Lee as the publishing manager, Jessica Lee as the graphic artist, Will Anderson as the developmental editor, and Rebecca Faith as the copyeditor. We literally could not have done this without you.

Our most heartfelt words of thanksgiving go to our spouses, children, and grandchildren for their unwavering patience, love, and support. Thank you for your gracious support.

Most of all, we are grateful for the grace of God. It is indeed by sola gratia.

CONTENTS

Dear Asian American Church …

Introduction

Embrace the Call

by Steve S. Chang

There is a crisis in the (Asian American) Church.

James Emery White calls it the "rise of the nones"[1]—a growing demographic that does not affiliate with any religion, which has grown from 16 percent in 2007 to 29 percent in 2021.[2] Jim Davis and Michael Graham call it the "great dechurching," stating, "We are currently in the middle of the largest and fastest religious shift in the history of our country. Approximately forty million (15 percent of American adults living today) have effectively stopped going to church, and most of this dechurching has happened in the past twenty-five years."[3] Americans are leaving the church in alarming numbers. What can we do?

Tim Keller proposes this trend could be reversed if the church in the United States embraces the global and multiethnic character of Christianity. Specifically, he points to the growth of the church in East Asia and the planting of hundreds of Chinese and Korean immigrant churches in New York, as signs of hope.[4] The single-race Asian American population is the fastest growing race in the country, projected to rise from 6.3 percent in 2022[5] to 9.1 percent by 2060.[6]

An Asian American Faith Crisis

Instead of flourishing and making an impact in the broader church, Asian Americans are also leaving the church in large numbers. Asian Americans who identified as Christians were 42 percent in 2012 but only 34 percent in 2022.[7] In fact, Graham believes that Asian Americans are dechurching faster than any other ethnic group. His research shows that Asian Americans are dechurching 40–50 percent faster than Whites and Blacks and at twice the rate of Hispanics.[8]

Instead of being the hope of revival, US-born Asian Americans (a.k.a. second+ generation) who are younger (median age of 19) compared to the foreign-born Asian Americans (median age of 34),[9] "are somewhat less likely than Asian Americans born elsewhere to say religion is very important in their lives."[10]

The False Hope of the American Church Dream

Many in the immigrant church are alarmed at the silent exodus of the second generation. Instead of staying in the immigrant church to lead the next generation, US-born, second-generation English-speaking Asian Americans have been conditioned to pursue the American church dream. At the core of this dream is the pressure to lay aside their ethnic identity and pursue true "Americanness," which essentially means being a cultural in our theology, ministry, hermeneutics, and homiletics. The underlying message is that ethnically neutral churches are more biblical, but ethnocentric churches are less so.

So, we mute our sermons from ethnic references to not offend non-Asians. We become critical, sometimes even ashamed, of the immigrant church for its overt ethnocentrism while pursuing White adjacency to make us feel legitimate.

While many assimilate into majority-culture and multiethnic churches, others long for spiritual communities where they can be their authentic selves. Feeling displaced, second-generation Asian Americans long for preachers who are honest about the pains and idols of their ethnic identity and history. They desire to be part of communities where they don't have to code-switch to feel at home.

An opportunity and a call exist for churches and leaders who are willing to contextualize the gospel to the emerging generation of Asian Americans. Those who step up have an opportunity to fill the spiritual vacuum and reverse the dechurching trend. Otherwise we may end up echoing the words of Judges 2:10, "And there arose another generation after them who did not know the LORD."

Vision of this Book

Many good works have been written by Asian Americans who are in academia, parachurches, and majority-culture spaces. Other practitioners from different theological streams have contributed greatly. We are grateful to learn from them all.

However, this book provides a space for church leaders who work in an Asian American context to share how they have contextualized the gospel for their congregations. Significantly, every contributor has spent the bulk of his/her ministry life in an Asian American context, whether in an English-speaking congregation attached to an immigrant church or in an independent Asian American church. They are bicultural, often bilingual, third-culture leaders committed to their local churches.

We believe we need Asian American pastors and churches to

speak with conviction and hope for the emerging generation and to infuse leaders with conviction, hope, and direction.

We believe that Asian American congregations are not only biblically permissible but also spiritually necessary.

We believe the unique strengths of the Asian American church should be stewarded, leveraged, and accentuated—not muted or assimilated.

We want to give the next generation a hard-earned road map for leading flourishing Asian American ministries so they can lead confidently and lean on those who have come before them.

Limitations and Definitions

Asian Americans are English-speaking second- or third-generation Americans of Asian heritage. An Asian American church is an English-speaking independent church or an English-speaking congregation attached to an immigrant church. We may also be referring to Asian American Christians in general, whether they are in an independent Asian American church, immigrant church, or majority-culture church.

We recognize that the experiences of many who are racially Asian may differ from those described here, including immigrants, adoptees, mixed race individuals, and the fourth+ generation of very early immigrants.

Although we believe many of the ideas and experiences included in this book are transferable, our contributors are exclusively of East Asian descent, and we do not purport to represent the whole of the Asian American Pacific Islander community. We do hope, however, to continue to learn from those from other parts of Asia (South Asia, Central Asia, West Asia, Southeast Asia, and Pacific Islands) because we have so much in common.

Although we are using the term *Asian American*, we believe the ideas discussed in this book also apply to the descendants of Asian immigrants in Canada, Australia, Europe, and other parts of the world.

The church in America has changed greatly in the last few decades. Twenty years ago, it was unfathomable to see Asian Americans leading large majority or multicultural churches. But today, many are doing exactly that. We fully recognize this book will be relevant for this season, but a new generation of writers, thinkers, and pastors will write another chapter twenty years from now. Our job is to give them a shoulder to stand on at this moment in time.

Theological Foundation

Our contributors come from various theological denominations and traditions. However, we all share the belief that the Bible is the inerrant Word of God and sufficient for life and godliness. We believe the gospel of Jesus Christ is the ultimate answer for all of man's problems and that it supersedes other helpful but limited disciplines, such as activism, psychology, or government. We believe the local church is the primary vehicle that God uses for his redemptive work.

Our Hope

Many Asian American churches spend too much time focusing on who we are *not* instead of who we are. What if we simply give thanks for who God has made us and steward our calling appropriately? What if we receive our Asian Americanness as a gift rather than a liability to overcome? Our goal is to help churches become all they are called to be.

Each contributor is a practitioner first. Some are theologians or academics, but their main contribution is their faithful ministry in Asian American contexts. Beyond reading them here, feel free to follow up by contacting them through the SOLA Network (https://sola.network).

You are likely reading this book because you care about the emerging generation of Asian Americans. Figuratively speaking, you are one of the elders who can lead this generation toward Christ. Together, let's normalize gospel-centered faith for the emerging generation of Asian Americans.

PART I

THE ASIAN IMMIGRANT CHURCH

1

Hidden Beauty: Finding Beauty and Opportunity in the Immigrant Church

by Faith Chang

Why does our church even exist?

The question lodged itself in my mind when I heard that a well-known church in Manhattan was looking to plant a church in our area.

My husband had only been pastoring at our church for about a year and we were already worn-out from issues common to small, immigrant churches. But this *other* church had a large, multiethnic ministry that attracted many of our Asian American peers—the kind of church I knew we never would be. So the question arose, not out of jealousy or territorialism as much as from deep discouragement. If this more effective, better-resourced church was going to start a church in our neighborhood, maybe we didn't need to be here. That was more than a decade ago. In the years since, God has answered my question hundreds of times. Week after week I have witnessed how— like a mustard seed in a field or yeast working through dough—God is expanding his kingdom through our church and others like it.

Perhaps like me, you're serving in an immigrant church, or maybe (also like me) you grew up in one. For over twenty years, I've served in Asian American ministry contexts and have had the privilege of being a *shi mu* (pastor's wife) at our current church for twelve years now. Through it all, I have become convinced that although Asian American immigrant churches have unique struggles, we also have an abundance of beauty to celebrate and opportunities to steward. Whether you're praying about a call to an immigrant church or curious to learn more about this corner of the church, this chapter is an invitation to praise God for the work he is doing in and among us. It is also a plea to pray with us that he would send more workers into our harvest fields.

Why Unique Blessings and Opportunities?

Before we begin to explore the unique blessings and opportunities God has entrusted to Asian American immigrant churches, it's helpful to consider why it can be hard for us to recognize these blessings and opportunities and why they are *unique* in the first place.

When I started serving at our church, I'd spent years soaking in teaching from the restless and reformed world, listening online to conference breakout sessions, and reading books about what it means to be a gospel-centered church. Many of those resources were helpful, but I didn't realize that my vision of the local church was being shaped by pastors in very different contexts from mine. Our church was a small group of believers, mostly from immigrant families, in New York City's forgotten outer borough, and as I listened to pastors from large well-resourced, majority-culture, city-based churches explain what a church should look like, it felt like we were doing things very wrong.

What's more, I was watching as peers chose to attend larger multiethnic or second-generation Asian churches, sometimes carrying bitterness or disdain for the immigrant church as they went. In retrospect, beneath my question of "Why do we even exist?" was a deep sense of being left behind and forgotten. God was working in those *other* churches that were doing things right, while our scrappy crew was barely holding it together.

The turning point came when God reminded me, *the church is the people of God.* God's church—his *ekklesia*—are his "called out" ones, people he has gathered to worship him in spirit and in truth. I'd heard church leaders talk about core values, ministry convictions, missional strategies, and church structure as if the local church was fundamentally those things. But the local church is fundamentally the *worshippers* that gather, each with his or her own spiritual gifts, experiences, culture, and needs. Attempting to replicate another church is like trying to follow instructions for constructing one Lego model when you're holding the pieces for a different set. Because no two churches are made up of the same individuals, churches will *necessarily* look different.

Thus, the lifeblood of every church must be the gospel of Jesus Christ, but what the gospel looks like fleshed out necessarily looks different in each community. God's glory and goodness is displayed in ways particular to each local body seeking to be Spirit-led and biblically faithful—even in small, largely unknown, Asian American immigrant churches like mine.

Finding Beauty in the Immigrant Church

So what are some of the unique blessings we might find in our immigrant churches? Your list will not be identical to mine. Still, there are some common themes that flow out of similarities in culture, shared needs, history, and immigrant experiences. Sometimes, recognizing a similar beauty elsewhere helps us recognize the beauty in our own churches, and I hope this list will prompt praise for what God is doing in your context.

The Beauty of Testimony

In Asian American immigrant churches, it's common to hear powerful testimonies from those who were once bound by fear of spirits, superstition, and false gods but who have been set free by the gospel. Because of this, we are privileged to witness the power of the gospel in ways similar to the New Testament church.

When the apostle Paul preached in Ephesus, sorcerers confessed their sins and burned their scrolls publicly (Acts 19:18–19). The homes of many of our people carry physical signs of a shift of allegiance from literal idols to the true and living God. I once came home to boxes filled with Chinese religious writings piled at our front door. My husband had been asked by a new believer to help discard them. My father-in-law (the founding pastor of our church) would smash idols—relinquished by new converts—in the church parking lot.

These testimonies are so precious because belief in Jesus is not just a matter of theological assent. Our church members recognize salvation as spiritual warfare and deliverance. Whether the gospel was introduced to our families in Asia or America, our stories include miraculous rescue from the darkness of shamanism, ancestor worship, Buddhism, and idolatry into God's kingdom of light.

We see the beauty of the gospel in our churches as children who had once been dedicated to false gods are baptized with their parents in the name of the Father, Son, and Holy Spirit. We see it as

unbelievers gripped with fear of evil spirits encounter church members who have been set free from the same bondage. Although secular
American culture denies the supernatural and treats Christianity as
one lifestyle choice among many, it is our privilege to declare how
God has tangibly brought us and our families "out of darkness into
his marvelous light" (1 Peter 2:9).

The Beauty of Legacy

The church in America often struggles to view Christianity beyond
our own setting of relative comfort. The cost of following Jesus is
hard to grasp when the barrier to entry seems so low, so we turn to
missionary biographies and stories about Christianity around the
world for examples of radical faith. One of the blessings of belonging
to an Asian American immigrant church is that these stories live and
breathe among us.

As a child, I attended church with a pastor who had survived
the Communist camps in China. Even in old age, he and his wife
prayed and read the Bible on their knees. Our churches have inherited the legacy of those who clung to Christ through persecution and
corporate suffering. Ours is the heritage of saints who trusted God
in government camps, through war, and as refugees in new lands.
Our pews hold those who refused to partake in ancestor worship in
Asia, which meant public shaming and even physical beatings. Others
continue to endure verbal and relational scorn from family members
because confessing Christ is seen as a rejection of family. The common
question from young people is: Should I get baptized, or should I
obey my non-Christian parents?

We have been entrusted with precious stories of costly faith,
and we strive to imitate the faith of our elders in sacrificial obedience,

bold evangelism, passionate prayer, and patient endurance. Their stories and presence in our lives disciple us in ways biographies and books cannot.

The Beauty of Global Missions and Evangelism

Another beautiful reality in Chinese American churches is the way the gospel does not just get passed *down* from generation to generation but works its way *up* and *across* them. Because of Communism, many Chinese believers only heard the gospel after immigrating to America. Our churches are full of people who are the first Christians in their families. Thus, it's common in our church for young children and youth to be actively praying and asking for prayer for their grandparents' salvations or the salvation of an unbelieving parent. Together, our church prays for those going back to their home countries to share the gospel with family members. Together, we rejoice when we hear reports of baptisms abroad. Church members visit the elderly parents of other church members during these trips to share the gospel with them too. All this infuses our church with a deep experiential conviction of our evangelistic and missional call.

Beyond evangelizing to family members, even though most of our churches are small, many have surprisingly robust ties to overseas missionary work. Asian American immigrant churches have largely avoided the debate of local ministry versus foreign missions because we know firsthand the need overseas and the debt we owe missionaries who first brought the gospel to Asia. Thus, global missions and evangelism are built into the DNA of most of our churches.

The Beauty of Church as Family

If you grew up in an immigrant church, you know what it's like to be surrounded by aunties and uncles who knew you (perhaps even when you didn't want to be known). Part of an Asian American immigrant church means experiencing the family of God in tangible ways.

Because of the nature of immigration, interdependence is a given in our communities. Those who have been in America longer help newer immigrants navigate education, health care, and government services. Without extended family nearby, church members pick up each other's kids from school and list one another as emergency contacts. In our churches, hospitality is less an event and looks more like a kind of permeability when it comes to home and relationships. Time together doesn't always have to be planned; people show up unannounced to help those in need. The assumption is that although people may not ask for help, it is our responsibility to be mindful and proactive in anticipating and meeting needs.

As it does in families, spiritual and relational care happens cross-generationally, especially in smaller immigrant churches. Aunties and uncles are Sunday school teachers and youth leaders. Older believers support teen and college short-term mission trips and write the names of the church's young people on their personal prayer lists. Children learn to take care of younger kids and sit with college students, who they refer to as their older brothers and sisters. Empty nesters invite singles over for meals, offering godly advice about job hunting or dating. In this familial context, life-on-life discipleship happens.

I've learned much from our churches on how to serve the stranger, the lonely, the sick, the dying, and those who are bereaved. Often I have been the recipient of this cross-generational whole-church care. Years ago, I sat in a prayer meeting as I was going through a miscarriage and a high schooler prayed for me. After the miscarriage, our church came around us, dropping off food and soup. I remember passing a grandma in the sanctuary after the

English service as she entered for the Chinese one. She put a hand on my shoulder and communicated her care with just one look. Jesus said that all people will know we are his disciples by our love (John 13:35), and the immigrant church demonstrates this love in a myriad of ways.

Finding Opportunity in the Immigrant Church

Over the years, my prayer for my church has changed from "Why are we here?" to "Lord, please send more workers!" While it may seem like immigrant churches have less opportunities for ministry because of our inherent constraints, there are many needs God has uniquely positioned us to meet, including evangelizing non-English speakers, discipling Asian American families, and supporting non-Asian immigrant churches.

Evangelism

It is projected that by 2055, Asian Americans will be the nation's largest immigrant group.[11] Given the continual flow of immigration from Asia, our churches have unique opportunities for evangelism. Newer immigrants are often willing to attend immigrant churches just to be with those who understand their language and culture. Many newcomers to our church were brought in by church members they connected with in the neighborhood or at local establishments simply because of their shared language and ethnic background. (One mother at our church regularly approaches other Chinese parents she meets at school and invites them to church!) In the past, I saw this as a liability—our churches can become more like cultural clubs than worshipping communities. But I've come to see it as a door for ministry that God is opening wide, providing natural relational bridges between our church and nonbelievers in the community.

Recently, my husband was the guest speaker for a Chinese church's retreat. A young man in the English congregation told him one reason he'd joined the church was because he wanted to bring his non-Christian mother. Though he worshipped with the English congregation, it was the Chinese speaking leaders who shared the gospel with her. Through them she came to faith before she passed away. This young man's story is not uncommon. Asian American Christians attending non-Asian or second-generation Asian churches often struggle when it comes to inviting their parents to church, and even those who don't end up moving to immigrant churches will sometimes reach out to our pastors asking for help sharing the gospel with non-English speakers.

Thus, there's a great opportunity to evangelize those who will never step into a majority culture or even a second-generation Asian church because of cultural and linguistic barriers. This also highlights how English-speaking congregations can minister to children coming to church for the first time as their parents explore faith.

Discipling First-Generation Christian Families

It's beautiful that many in our congregation are the first Christians in their homes, but this also poses an inherent challenge. Asian American immigrant parents already struggle to navigate life in America while raising kids who are growing up in a culture different from their own. Add to the challenge of generational and cultural gaps the call to raise children in Christ. Having grown up in non-Christian homes, they have no frame of reference for what a Christian family looks like. Thus, there is a need for a special kind of discipleship for the whole family.

Those of us serving in the English ministries of our churches, particularly with children and youth, feel this need deeply. With children and parents both learning about Christianity for the first time, there are a plethora of opportunities for discipleship. As we serve the children of immigrants, God gives us opportunities to pray with, counsel, and disciple parents who attend the non-English services. These parents not only need to grow as disciples of Christ, but they also need help seeing parenting from a biblical perspective. They seek practical wisdom for how to discipline their children, how to understand current cultural issues, and how to deal with the temptations their kids face in school.

Many immigrant parents in our churches are desperate for guidance on how to talk to, relate with, pray for, and raise their kids. They need modeling, shepherding, and instruction from mature believers who will disciple them with cultural understanding, compassion, and biblical wisdom.

Serving Non-Asian Immigrants

One surprising opportunity God has given our church is serving Christians from non-Asian immigrant contexts. For example, children from a nearby Coptic church have attended our VBS. Their children are American born, but their parents are relatively new immigrants. These parents expressed their concerns about raising their kids in the faith when America presents different challenges than the persecution they experienced in Egypt. Although our experiences were not identical, our church could minister to these parents because we understood the difficulty of intergenerational cultural differences while ministering to second-generation youth. Our church has also had opportunities to serve those in our community whose families emigrated from Europe. By his grace, God has used our experience as minority and immigrant Christians to serve the church cross-culturally.

The Beauty and Opportunity of Loving for God's Glory

Ultimately, the beauty and opportunity of Asian American immigrant churches is found in the people God calls us to love and the glory of the One who chooses "what is foolish in the world to shame the wise; … what is weak in the world to shame the strong; … what is low and despised in the world, even things that are not, to bring to nothing things that are, so that no human being might boast in the presence of God" (1 Cor. 1:27–29). Learning to love God and love people in largely hidden places is deeply good for our souls.

If you have been called to an immigrant church that doesn't look like much to the world or even in your own eyes, know that you have not been left behind. God is the God of hidden places, small things, despised things, and things that "are not." He takes notice of you and your church family. He is among you. He loves you. Your labor is not in vain because *he* is at work. God is doing beautiful things in our churches, and we exist because there is work yet to be done.

2

Unraveling Diversity: The Surprising Gift
of the Asian Heritage Church

by Enoch Y. Liao

"My church is so messed up." The pastor sitting across from me was
in tears because his Asian immigrant church of fewer than seventy
people was experiencing serious conflict. He was afraid his church
would split between the older generation born overseas and the
younger American-born generation.

"Our church is so small, we're all the same, and we still can't get
along. But that church down the road with thousands of people is so
diverse and yet they can work well together. What's wrong with my
church? What's wrong with my leadership?"

Have you ever had such thoughts? Have you wondered how
a church made up of the same race can have so much interpersonal
conflict? Have you looked at larger churches which seem to get along
despite being more diverse? Why does a small immigrant Asian
church seem to have disproportionately more conflict and turmoil
than larger multiethnic churches?

Some people come to strong conclusions about these questions. Many of those conclusions seem to blame the Asian immigrant culture of those churches. "There's just something wrong with the Chinese church," or "I will never go to another Korean church," or "I've given up on the Vietnamese church." "After all, if a church under eighty people, full of only Koreans or Chinese, can't get along, then maybe something is seriously wrong with the Asian cultures of those churches."

Is there *really* something fundamentally wrong with such churches due to their Asian culture? Or is there another explanation for the seemingly high level of conflict and tension in Asian American churches?

How Diverse Can a Church Full of Asians Be?

I propose that we take another look at the supposed diversity of various churches. I hope to show that so-called monolithic Asian American churches aren't so monolithic and that churches touted as diverse may not be as diverse as people say they are.

Asian churches in America are more diverse than people realize. And why is that important? Because if Asian American churches are more diverse than people realize, instead of criticizing them for how much conflict they experience, we may instead praise God for how well these diverse churches get along! And perhaps we would feel less discouragement and self-loathing about our churches.

Are there reasons to be encouraged by how God is working in these churches?

Is some of the criticism unhelpful and even unjustified?

Instead of disparaging Asian immigrant churches, can celebrate how God is working among them?

Are Asian American churches in fact some of the most diverse churches in America?

What Do I Mean by "Diversity"?

For the purposes of this chapter, I will define *diversity* as differences among groups of people that can create friction or barriers to communication, relationships, and ministry. This definition may seem to imply that diversity is only negative. That's not my intention. Diversity can be wonderful and ideally adds richness to our churches and lives. But to experience those blessings requires patience, understanding, effort, and grace.

People tend to define diversity quite narrowly in the United States. I hear people speak of diversity in two common ways. Often the word *diverse* usually means racial or ethnic difference. For example, when someone tells me a church or a team is diverse, they usually mean the people are from racial backgrounds different from the dominant culture.

Outside the evangelical world in the secular marketplace and culture, a second way people often use the term *diversity* has to do with gender.

Scripture does acknowledge those two types of diversity, but are race and gender the only types of diversity we see in Scripture? Are there other diversities described in the Bible?

I believe there are more than two types of diversity. I also believe that other types of diversity may be more profound in the challenges they present.

A Diversity of Diversities in the Bible

I see at least seven different types of diversity in the Bible. These types of diversity are complex (and, in my experience, often controversial).

Each of these diversities presents the church with both challenges and opportunities. In the Asian American church, we have focused on the opportunities and potential benefits of diversity, but I think that the Asian American church has glossed over the challenges it presents. In fact, my argument is that many Americans—both Asian and otherwise—have underestimated the profound challenges of diversity in Asian immigrant churches in the United States.

Let's start with the two types of diversity we have already discussed: racial diversity and gender diversity.

Racial/Ethnic Diversity

Without getting into the complex discussion about the difference between race and ethnicity, I think most would readily agree that racial/ethnic difference creates friction in ministry.

Notice how the apostle Paul emphasizes unity in spite of racial differences. "For there is no distinction between Jew and Greek (Gentile); for the same Lord is Lord of all, bestowing his riches on all who call on him. For 'everyone who calls on the name of the Lord will be saved'" (Rom. 10:12–13).

Throughout the book of Luke, we see the animosity and hostility between Jewish disciples and gentile Samaritans (e.g., see Luke 9:51–56; 17:11–17). John's gospel states, "For Jews have no dealings with Samaritans" (John 4:9b).

Although racial and ethnic diversity can present the church with opportunities, Scripture nonetheless acknowledges that racial and ethnic differences can lead to incredible conflict and strife.

Gender Diversity

In our cultural moment, diversity is often associated with sexual orientation and gender identity. These topics merit their own discussion.

For this section, however, I merely want to show that gender difference has always been a barrier to gospel communication and ministry.

Consider the account of Jesus talking with the Samaritan woman at the well. It's significant this woman was a Samaritan, but the gospel writer emphasizes her *gender*. The mere fact that Jesus converses with a woman unsettles his disciples: "Just then his disciples came back. They marveled that he was talking with a woman…" (John 4:27a).

In New Testament times, women were seen as lesser than men. While we've seen *some* progress toward valuing women in modern life, there is still much work to be done. Tragically, it's often the case that gender differences, which are meant to be a gift we celebrate, unearth our sinful tendency to elevate some at the expense of others.

After considering these first two types of diversity—ethnicity and gender—let's look at five more, which I believe can be even more challenging to navigate.

Generational Diversity

Third, we see *generational diversity*. In Luke 18:15–17, parents brought their children to Jesus so he could bless them, but the disciples hindered them from meeting Jesus. Apparently, the disciples considered children unworthy of their master's time. Jesus responded by inviting his followers to imitate children when it comes to discipleship: "Whoever does not receive the kingdom of God like a child shall not enter it."

Another endearing example of age difference presenting a challenge is in Acts 12, when a slave girl named Rhoda tried to tell adults in a prayer meeting that God had answered their prayers. The believers were praying for the Lord to deliver the apostle Peter from prison, and when Rhoda tells them Peter is at the gate, the adults tell her she's out of her mind (Acts 12:13–15). If the adults had been willing to believe Rhoda, they may have been quicker to celebrate the Lord's answer to their prayers.

In Scripture, Paul explains how intergenerational households should honor one another: "Do not rebuke an older man but encourage him as you would a father" (1 Tim. 5:1). If Paul felt the need to offer this instruction, it seems reasonable to conclude that younger men may have offered harsh and sharp rebukes to the older men. In the Bible and in our day, generations can be quick to write off one another. Generational diversity should be celebrated, but generational values, preferences, and tastes also present significant challenges.

National/Political Diversity

Fourth, we see *national and political diversity*. In Matthew 10:2–4 we find a list of the twelve disciples of Jesus. Consider two of these disciples in particular: Matthew the "tax collector" and Simon "the Zealot." The Zealots were a group of Jewish extremists who opposed Roman occupation and oppression, and tax collectors were Jews who aligned with the Roman government to extract taxes from their own people. To the Zealots, this was tantamount to being a traitor to both God and country. Thus, when Jesus later shows kindness to a notorious tax collector named Zacchaeus, it shocks the crowds (Luke 19:1–10).

In today's world, consider the divide between progressive and conservative, left and right, Democrat and Republican. Politics divide people, even within the same family!

Socioeconomic Diversity

Fifth, we can identify *socioeconomic diversity* (sometimes called "class diversity"), seen in Jesus's parable about a Pharisee and tax collector (Luke 18:9–14). These two figures had different moral and socioeconomic standings. Clearly one of them (the Pharisee) despised the other (the tax collector). Imagine the challenges in the early church when these diverse individuals joined the same church. The epistle of James notes tensions between rich and poor; apparently, favoritism was shown to the former (James 2:1–7).

Beyond rich and poor, class diversity includes barriers between slave and master, Roman citizen and subject, ruler and servant. Class, slavery, and socioeconomic differences create profound barriers and conflict among people. This type of diversity is one we use to excuse barriers between ourselves and others in the church. Consider the legacy of slavery and the divide between rich and poor in our country today, and we can see how this diversity creates challenges.

Language Diversity

The sixth type of diversity I see in Scripture is *language diversity*. In Genesis chapter 11, God himself causes a division of language among the peoples. This language confusion causes the people to disperse from one another and abandon their concerted project to construct a tower. In the New Testament, when Jews of many languages gathered together in Jerusalem for Pentecost, the language barrier is so challenging that the Holy Spirit enables everyone to hear gospel preaching in their own language.

Having sat through hundreds of bilingual or trilingual worship services, I would gladly welcome the ability to interpret everyone in the room! To this day, the challenge of language acquisition plagues not only gospel communication but also important areas of life such as employment, communication in families, and education. Language diversity is one of the most challenging parts of attending my church, which offers worship services in three languages, but the broader American evangelical church rarely seems to consider this.

In Boston, I often meet with other Christian leaders who declare that they are planning a "citywide" event for Christians. While I appreciate the intention and effort to gather Christians from across our city, I often ask myself, "Should we really call this unity event a citywide endeavor if we only offer it in a single language?"

Cultural Diversity

In my view, people underestimate the impact of culture on communication, relationships, and philosophy of ministry.

The story of the selection of the seven deacons in Acts 6:1–7 is often described as a conflict between Jewish and Greek Christians. The Greeks complained that the Jewish Christians were neglecting their widows in the daily distribution of food. In response, the apostles appointed seven men to address this matter. This passage is cited as a case in which the Spirit enabled the early church to resolve heated conflict between two racial groups. Except that this is not a conflict between two racial groups. This is conflict between members of the same racial/ethnic group. A complaint arose by the Hellenists against the Hebrews (Acts 6:1). Most Bible translators note that the Hellenists were ethnically Jewish but culturally Greek. In other words, this is conflict between Jews who are from two cultural backgrounds, not two racial groups. To put it another way, the first major conflict in the early church was sparked by cultural diversity, compounded by linguistic diversity, and probably related to political and socioeconomic diversity.

A Typical Asian Immigrant Church

Now that we've considered a more diverse set of diversities, consider the typical Asian immigrant church in America today. Many evangelicals may look at such churches and see one ethnic people group. They may conclude that such churches are monolithic, full of people that are basically the same. But let's take another look. An immigrant church may have people of mostly the same ethnic descent, but what about the other types of diversity? Consider a typical church like mine, which is a Chinese heritage church.

Consider linguistic diversity. There may be two or even three languages used in church. Consider the complexity that creates for leadership, planning, prayer, or combined worship services.

There may be multiple generations in the same church. You might see people in their seventies who speak only Chinese, middle-aged people who are somewhat bilingual, and the children of those couples who may only speak English.

In my Chinese heritage church, political diversity abounds. We have Republicans, Democrats, and independents. Beyond diversity over American politics, you will find diverse views about issues involving China, Hong Kong, Taiwan, and Tibet. All these diverse views may be held by thoughtful, intelligent, informed, and passionate people.

My church is also culturally diverse, comprising Chinese people from China, Taiwan, Hong Kong, the United States, and other places.

We have class diversity. Some attendees are low-income, blue-collar workers with little to no education. Some are graduates from the most prestigious colleges and universities doing cutting edge work in science. Our congregants work in government offices, finance companies, hair salons, public schools, casinos, tech start-ups, and spas.

Imagine what it is like to be in a leadership meeting with such diversity. Do we use direct, candid language, or should we practice deference to one another? Imagine planning a worship service amid such diversity. What songs would you choose for congregational singing? Imagine the myriad of ministries needed for such a full range of ages, life stages, and socioeconomic backgrounds. Imagine trying to come up with a sermon illustration to fit the lived experience of various attendees. Even if I preach the same Bible passage in different worship services, I have to come up with different illustrations and applications for the various audiences based on age, language, culture, and class.

Yes, most of the people in my church are Chinese, but all things considered, I would wager my church is highly diverse, considering the various types of diversity we've discussed.

What about that new church in town that is diverse? Sure, it may be racially diverse with people from various cultural backgrounds. But within the context of leadership and structure, such a church is often monogenerational, monoclass, monolingual, and monocultural.

The Call and Challenge of Diversity

The point of this chapter is not to see who wins a contest of diversity Olympics. I'm not making a case that every church must be more or less diverse in various ways, nor am I criticizing any church for its lack of diversity. I also acknowledge that although diversity presents many challenges—often underestimated—it also presents opportunities.

The point is to help people understand that in a typical Asian heritage church in America, there may be far more diversity than you realize. And if there's far more diversity, there may be that much more complexity to deal with. And more complexity means more challenges.

So a leader in a typical Asian or immigrant heritage church faces more diversity and complexity in church than is apparent on the surface. Perhaps some of the struggle, tension, and conflict is due to a higher degree of diversity than is normally acknowledged. Instead of wondering why your church is so messed up even though "we are all the same," consider how gracious God has been to enable your church to work together despite significant diversity.

Perhaps one reason your church struggles with communication and conflict is not because of your ethnic heritage but because of the incredible amount of complexity stemming from the underappreciated amount of diversity. Of course, it is sin and our fallen nature that takes the challenges of diversity and produces quarrels (James 4:1). Embrace the fact that serving in an immigrant church in America means serving in an incredibly complex and diverse setting.

As a church member or leader, maybe you don't feel called to deal with a high level of complexity. Conversely, perhaps you feel a burden to be a part of a church that embodies the beauty and challenge of such diversity for the sake of Christ and the gospel. Either way, I hope God uses the observations in this chapter to bring perspective on our churches. May the Spirit help us leverage the rich diversity of our churches, and may the Lord use these insights to nurture hope for the Lord's work in our churches.

The Spirit of God calls us where he chooses. If God has called you to serve in an Asian immigrant church, embrace the complexity and diversity. Joyfully depend on God for strength to love and serve his church.

3

Every Tribe and Tongue: The Challenges and Blessings of Multilingual Churches

by Jason M. Tarn

"Next Sunday we're having combined service."

Cue the sighs and eye rolls. For a teenager growing up in an immigrant church, the idea of worshipping with your parents and the rest of the immigrant congregation is dreadfully boring. Not only can you expect the songs to be outdated, but they'll also be sung in a language you barely understand. "But, don't worry, the sermon will be translated." Great. That just makes it twice as long and half as interesting.

I started attending a Chinese heritage church when I was a teenager. I remember suffering through combined services while mentally checking out. My Chinese was poor, and because my immigrant parents were non-Christians, there was no spiritual jargon spoken at home. My comprehension of Chinese was equivalent to a pagan first grader. I spent most of my time in combined services counting the ceiling lights. Then I'd move on to tiles.

Beyond Sunday mornings, the difficult task of leading an immigrant church is exacerbated when attendees speak multiple languages. Between the different congregations, there are clashing cultures and competing interests. Combined with the lack of a shared language and it's the perfect recipe for distrust and division. Those serving in immigrant churches sometimes fantasize about how nice it would be if everyone spoke the same language. Imagine how much deeper our fellowship might be. Imagine how much more efficient and clear our meetings would be. No one would have to translate. No one would have to resort to a second language. We could all speak in our native tongue and reduce all the confusion and miscommunication.

This is why many see the multiple languages in an immigrant church as a liability—a nuisance to endure; a problem to solve. But *what if* the multilingual nature of an immigrant church is actually one of its enduring strengths? What if it gives the immigrant church an advantage in displaying the unifying power of the gospel?

Much is written these days about diversity in the church. We're encouraged to pursue congregational diversity to display gospel unity. But in this well-intentioned pursuit, many churches are operating with a truncated view of diversity—thinking merely in terms of ethnicity or race. But there are other forms of diversity to be experienced. Cultural. Generational. Political. Socioeconomic. And, of course, linguistic.

I would argue that experiencing unity in a multilingual church is just as challenging as it is in a multiethnic church. This becomes more apparent as we develop a biblical theology of language. Where did the diversity of languages come from? Why is there not one universal common language? And is that the goal? Is that what we will experience one day in heaven? Will we all be speaking one common heavenly tongue?

Answering these questions not only helps us appreciate the immigrant church—it opens our eyes to the all-surpassing power of the gospel to unite a people divided by language. Genesis 11:1–9 tells the story of the Tower of Babel, in which we are confronted with the power of a common language, God's judgment by multiplying language, and his redemption of all languages.

The Power of a Common Language

It's so much easier to work with people when you all speak a common language. Things get done faster. Church meetings in which you or others are asked to switch to a second language tend to get bogged down and dragged out. More is accomplished when we share the same tongue. The Tower of Babel confirms this. Genesis 11 shows how a common language enables great innovation and collaboration.

In the beginning, Genesis reveals that everyone was made in the same divine image (Gen. 1:27) and spoke the same language (Gen. 11:1). The people settle in the land of Shinar and build a new city and a tower. The location is an interesting choice. The typical building blocks for ancient Near Eastern structures—stone and mortar—are not naturally available in that region. So, the people must innovate. Aided by a shared language, they figure out how to use baked bricks instead of stone and bitumen in place of mortar. A common language propels them toward a common goal.

So, you would think their shared language would contribute to a shared unity of faith in the Lord. However, sin entered the world (Gen. 3) and corrupted human collaboration. A common language certainly united humanity, but sadly, it united them in rebellion against God. "Then they said, 'Come, let us build ourselves a city and a tower with its top in the heavens, and let us make a name for

ourselves, lest we be dispersed over the face of the whole earth.'"
(Gen. 11:4).

I can sympathize with their desire to huddle rather than disperse.
Everyone speaks the same language. They work well as a group. Why
would they part ways? It all seems sensible and innocent until you read
Genesis 11 in the context of Genesis 9:1, where God commanded
humanity to "be fruitful and multiply and fill the earth." Apparently,
their mandate was to spread out and populate the planet, to fill the
earth with the praise and knowledge of the Lord—which meant their
decision to stay put was an act of rebellion.

The people were blessed with a common language. They had the
power and potential to do so much for God's glory and name. But
because of sin, they were too busy trying to preserve their own glory
and establish their own name.

The Judgment by Multiplying Languages

In the next scene, God responded to their sinful rebellion. He judged
them by multiplying their languages. For many reading this story, this
is surprising. Those who grow up speaking more than one language
often appreciate being multilingual. It can be jarring to discover that
all the various languages were born out of rebellion. We rightly feel
tension. Again, our experience of the multilingual immigrant church
confirms this. The presence of multiple languages is treated as an
inconvenience at best and a threat to unity at worst. The confusion and
miscommunication we experience often feels like a form of judgment.

It's ironic when the text says the Lord had to come down to see
this puny thing they were building.

And the Lord came down to see the city and the tower, which
the children of man had built. And the Lord said, "Behold,

they are one people, and they have all one language, and this is only the beginning of what they will do. And nothing that they propose to do will now be impossible for them." (Gen. 11:5–6)

So God comes down to stop them. Not because he's worried they'll become unstoppable, but because he knows they'll never stop in their rebellion. If he doesn't act now, there's no telling how bad they'll get. They'll eventually destroy themselves and all of creation. So, God comes down and confuses their speech.

> "Come, let us go down and there confuse their language, so that they may not understand one another's speech." So the Lord dispersed them from there over the face of all the earth, and they left off building the city. Therefore its name was called Babel, because there the Lord confused the language of all the earth. And from there the Lord dispersed them over the face of all the earth. (Gen. 11:7–9)

No longer possessing a common language, they could no longer collaborate. They wanted to make a name for themselves, but they couldn't even pronounce each other's names. They wanted to avoid dispersion, but now they're scattered over the earth. This is God's judgment.

What does this mean for us? Does it mean that all the various languages on earth were born in sinful disobedience? Partly, yes. That is what Babel teaches. But are they inherently bad? Is the presence of multiple languages counter to God's will? Does he plan to reunite us around one common language? Will he restore us as one tribe with one tongue? The Bible's answer is clearly no. Beautifully, God in his sovereignty uses our sinful rebellion to accomplish his greater plans.

The Redemption of all Languages

To see how this works, we must read this story of Babel within the larger narrative that unfolds from the Old to the New Testament. As we do, we discover his plan to redeem every language on the earth.

By Genesis 11:9, the situation is bleak. People are finally filling the earth, but humanity is fractured. Their unity is gone. Humanity has splintered into many tribes and tongues. Then in Genesis 12, we're introduced to a man named Abraham—a man to whom God makes great promises. The rest of the Bible tells the story of how God keeps this promise to make a great name and a great nation out of Abraham and his family.

But that story is continually sidelined by the same sinfulness dramatically illustrated at Babel. Because there are a thousand tongues in the world, there also are a thousand ways to worship falsely and a thousand ways to praise false gods in a native tongue. That plays out in the rest of the Old Testament. False worship covers the face of all the earth. But the prophets hint that this will not always be so. In Zephaniah 3:9, the Lord foretells a time when the speech of the nations will be changed: "For at that time I will change the speech of the peoples to a pure speech, that all of them may call upon the name of the LORD and serve him with one accord."

You might assume that means everyone will speak one language, but it's not the case. The emphasis is on the *purity* of their speech in contrast to the false worship of the nations. God is saying that, one day, he will do something that leads all the peoples on the earth to pure worship. We'll be reunited to serve God with one accord.

As the storyline of Scripture continues into the New Testament, we meet a son of Abraham. His name is Jesus. And we discover that he is God incarnate. Once again, God comes down to visit a city to see what its inhabitants built. This city was called Jerusalem, and the temple built there had become a shameful den of thieves (Matt. 21:13).

Five days later, this Jesus was led out of Jerusalem's gates with a cross on his back (Heb. 13:12). Again, we see punishment for sin, but this time it's Jesus who takes the punishment *for* humanity. He gets thrown out of the city so his people can stay. Jesus is exiled and killed, so that sinners can be restored to God and receive new life.

At Babel, things went off track. But now, through the life, death, and resurrection of Christ, we are brought back on track with God's plan of redemption.

After Christ's ascension, God comes down again, this time in the person of the Holy Spirit. The disciples were gathered on the day of Pentecost, when suddenly the Spirit fell on them and they began to speak in foreign tongues. Acts 2:7–8 says those in Jerusalem were "amazed and astonished, saying, 'Are not all these who are speaking Galileans? And how is it that we hear, each of us in his own native language?'"

Significantly, not everyone begins to speak and understand the same language. Instead, the Spirit enables everyone to hear the gospel proclaimed in their native tongue. Peter stands up and explains that these events are a sign of the last days, predicted by prophets like Zephaniah, who spoke of a time when all nations call on the name of the Lord with pure speech (see Zeph. 3:9). This is how the story of Babel finds its resolution in the events of Pentecost. Unity was lost at Babel. It was restored at Pentecost. Confusion was sown at Babel. Understanding was recovered at Pentecost. Pentecost is not the reversal of Babel, as some scholars suggest, because God's people were not restored to one common language.

When we get to heaven, we won't speak one language. In Revelation, John's vision of heaven includes "a great multitude that no one could number, from every nation, from all tribes and peoples and languages, standing before the throne and before the Lamb" (Rev. 7:9). Apparently, in the future we will sing and worship the Lamb in our native tongue. It's more accurate to say that Pentecost *redeems* the effects of Babel. We won't go back to sharing a common language because God has given the church an even greater source of unity—something stronger than a shared tongue.

Language is a powerful unifying force, but according to God's unfolding plan, from Pentecost onward, the redeemed people of God will be unified—not by a common language or culture—but by a common faith and Spirit. There is *one gospel* in which we all trust and *one Spirit* in whom we all share (see Eph. 4:4). Christian unity doesn't depend on choosing and using one language.

Hope for the Multilingual Church

This is where a church like mine fits into the story. Babel finds its narrative resolution in the events of Pentecost, but its contemporary expression can be found in the multilingual immigrant church. Yes, it's difficult to navigate multiple languages in a church. Good intentions literally get lost in translation. Sometimes we're tempted to think it would be easier if the various language groups just went their separate ways.

Perhaps what we treat as a nuisance and liability is actually a unique strength. Instead of complaining that our immigrant church lacks the unifying power of a shared tongue, we can celebrate our multiple languages to show the world there's something stronger keeping us together. Though we speak many languages, we won't be dispersed like at Babel. Because, as at Pentecost, we are undeniably unified by one gospel and Spirit.

If you worship in an immigrant church, I hope you've been encouraged to see your church with fresh eyes—to see its multilingual nature as a beautiful form of diversity and an expression of deep unity only possible through the gospel. If your church has a combined service, it's a signpost of the coming kingdom. It's a foretaste of heavenly worship, where we'll all be singing the same song of the redeemed, each in our native tongue.

The next time you sit through a translated sermon, give thanks. When you stand with worshippers from another congregation, singing songs you don't know very well in a language you don't speak very well, rejoice! As you take communion alongside those with whom you are divided by language, remember you are united by faith.

4

Safe Spaces: Providing Counsel in the Asian Immigrant Church

by Monica M. Kim

Years ago, I was walking down the hallway of my Korean immigrant–American church where I served on the pastoral staff. A mother of a high school teen quietly approached me. Eyes downcast, in a soft and quiet voice, she expressed how embarrassed and ashamed she felt as she asked for help. She did not want to burden me but felt she had nowhere else to turn. Her son was having trouble at school, and his teachers and the administrators of the high school had been reaching out to meet with her and her husband. She had been avoiding this meeting for a while but no longer could. She asked me to help her by attending this meeting. Her command of the English language was very limited, and she was afraid of what the school might say about her son.

She also shared that her husband was very angry and ashamed of their son, even calling him *byungshin* often. This is a Korean curse word that is difficult to translate, but when used in anger, it essentially means "idiot." I was sad and brokenhearted for the son, the mother, and even this father who was ashamed of his son. I agreed to attend the meeting with her, affirming the courage it took to seek help. In my heart and mind, I wanted her to sincerely know that Jesus—our Savior, the King of Kings—was not ashamed of her family. Avoiding shame and maintaining some semblance of honor in our Asian church community is a cultural value. However, I wanted to point her to our God, who through Christ—in his death, resurrection, ascension, and reign—has covered our shame and clothed us with honor.

I asked the mother for some more details about her son and the trouble he was having at school. She explained that he was failing classes, and at home he would often stay in his room behind closed doors. She struggled to have normal conversations with him. He claimed to see things around him she could not see. He would often talk about how God gave him power to be like God. As a professional psychologist, biblical counselor, and local church pastor, I recognized the issue her son was likely struggling with.

I went to the high school meeting planning to be her advocate and cultural–linguistic liaison. The mom and I met in front of the school (the father did not attend). We went in together and I introduced myself and the mom to the team of administrators and teachers. From the outset, they compassionately expressed how they'd tried many times to meet with the parents in hopes of providing their son with options and resources, given that he was clearly showing signs and symptoms of schizophrenia in class. This was preventing him from meeting academic goals and getting the kind of education he deserved. The school team seemed to know how important it was to engage this mother with kindness, compassion, and honor. Now, I won't get into the details of the plans agreed upon, but I do want to highlight how, in this kind and compassionate environment, the mom was able to accept the help her son needed.

Loving, Biblical Counsel

This experience demonstrates that, as Asian Americans, we minister in an honor and shame culture. In this culture, families or individuals sometimes allow perpetual suffering to continue rather than receive help. I am purposely using the word *counsel* to distinguish it from *counseling*. Counseling, in our American culture, typically entails meeting with a professional or trained lay counselor to receive help or guidance for specific troubles. As a psychologist and biblical counselor, I've noticed that the Korean immigrant–American church (to which I've belonged for most of my life) doesn't usually engage in this type of organized counseling. Noticeably, this is changing among second- and third-generation Asian Americans. However, for many Asian immigrant–American churchgoers, setting up an organized counseling ministry is culturally incongruent.

This doesn't mean your hands are tied. Pastors and church leaders of Asian American immigrant churches can provide counsel in the church, socially contextualized around the values of honor and shame, through a gospel-centered approach. Although much can be said about counseling in various cultural contexts, this chapter focuses on how to counsel in an Asian immigrant honor and shame culture. Pastors and church leaders need to consider the importance of how intentional, loving, biblical counsel can be provided in the context of an honor and shame culture.

Honor and Shame Culture

When defining any honor and shame culture, it's vital to start with Scripture. Mankind is created on the sixth day as the pinnacle of God's creation (Gen. 1:26–31), and only mankind is given the honor of being made in the image of God (v. 26). Strikingly, Genesis 2:25 says, "the man and his wife were both naked and were not ashamed." Before Adam and Eve disobeyed God's command, there was no shame.

Tragically, after they sin by eating from the tree of the knowledge of good and evil, they realize they are naked and frantically try to cover themselves with fig leaves, then hide in shame when God approaches (Gen. 3: 6–10). These cowering humans, ashamed and avoiding God's gaze, stand in stark contrast to Adam and Eve in their original state, when they were naked and *not ashamed*. From this moment forward, all people have experienced shame, whether ancient or modern, Eastern or Western.

Although mankind's relationship with God was severed because of the fall, mankind *still* bears the image of God. God shows his compassion by seeking them out in love, even when Adam and Eve cover themselves and hide. God spells out the results of sin, then he makes Adam and Eve "garments of skins" (Gen. 3:21) and compassionately clothes them—foreshadowing our being clothed with Christ through baptism as children of God through faith (see Gal. 3:26–27). Although shame, brokenness, and death resulted from the fall, through Christ's life, death, and resurrection we are clothed with everlasting righteousness and honor.

While we cherish these gospel truths, we still experience and struggle with shame as individuals and people groups. It is commonly understood that honor–shame is one of the central values of Asian cultures, even though the distinctives of this value vary widely among the Asian cultures. Honor is highly valued, and shame is generally avoided. I say "generally" because in some cases shame is viewed as neutral or positive. For example, shame sometimes prompts change—

it's a guide and guard for moral living—that can bring honor to the family or community. According to KnowledgeWorkx, "In an Honor-Shame–oriented culture, the honor of the family, honor of the tribe, your village, city, the honor of the nation you represent—honor is key. And the avoidance of shame is crucial in the process of advancing and preserving honor. Both honor and shame are seen as neutral in terms of how you deploy them."[12]

Joined to this overarching definition of an honor and shame culture, one's place in the collective or communal society is significant. Honor is related to how a person behaves within one's position in ways the group values; and shame is related to one behaving in ways that are incongruent from what the group values, given their position. From this general definition, it would be reasonable to say that this is how Asian immigrant–American churches are organized socioculturally— through this relationally interdependent honoring of one another, the group, and the church and avoiding shame, within one's position in the church and society. If we remember the mother I mentioned at the beginning of this chapter, although she and her family were experiencing a severe struggle, they avoided shame by avoiding any communication with the school. When she could no longer avoid the shame, even though it would bring dishonor to the family, she quietly disclosed her need for help with an authority figure in the church she believed could help, in a respectful manner with a posture of shame. She also disclosed this in a way that would not bring dishonor to the larger church.

Contextualizing Counsel in an Asian Immigrant–American Church

Considering the honor–shame dynamics in the Asian American church, wise, godly, grace-abounding counsel is greatly needed.

The ancient Near Eastern cultures or Mediterranean societies of the Bible lived in an honor–shame culture, and to give and receive counsel was an integral part of life. In Scripture, counsel involves giving and receiving guidance in a purposeful, deliberate manner, which leads to wise, godly living. It is one very significant way the Lord sanctifies us.

In light of honor–shame dynamics in the Asian American church, wise, godly, grace-abounding counsel is greatly needed. It is well known that the ancient Near Eastern cultures or Mediterranean societies of the Bible lived in an honor–shame culture and to give and receive counsel was an integral part of the culture, as it is with all people. When we examine the four Hebrew words in the Old Testament [i.e., תַּחְבֻּלָה (tachbulah), עֵצָה ʿ(etsah), סוֹד (cowd), יָעַץ (yaats)] and the one Greek word in the New Testament [i.e., βουλεύω (bouleuó)], which are translated as "counsel," we find that in Scripture, counsel involves giving and receiving guidance in a purposeful, deliberate manner, which leads to wise godly living. It is one very significant way the Lord sanctifies us. Furthermore, to provide counsel involves developing a trusted relationship with another person, much like a friend, with the goal of mutual listening, clarifying, and planning together how to align one's life in the particulars (e.g., relationship with God and people, painful situations, future plans, etc.) with God's gospel truths. Counseling in Scripture is not about an organized set of procedures or structure; it's about giving and receiving guidance in a relationship of trust, safety, privacy, closeness, careful listening, and collaboration.

So, as Asian Americans in an honor and shame culture, how can we cultivate a robust counsel culture in our churches?

Examine Your Own Character

Creating a church culture in which guidance and change can happen starts with the character of the pastor or leader. In this regard, as leaders in positions of authority, our character matters—especially when leading others through sensitive issues like suffering, illness, and sin. Scripture calls us to grow in character lest we become ineffective or unfruitful (2 Peter 1:5–8). Furthermore, 1 Timothy 1:5 states, "[But the goal of our instruction] is love that issues from a pure heart and a good conscience and a sincere faith."

Research in Christian psychology reveals that a counselor's character strength and virtues contribute to the effectiveness of a counselor or one who is providing counsel.[13] Thus, it is necessary for pastors and church leaders to reflect deeply on their character qualities and consider how we ourselves, because of Christ, have put on "compassionate hearts, kindness, humility, meekness, and patience, bearing with one another and, if one has a complaint against another, forgiving each other; … And above all these put on love, which binds everything together in perfect harmony" (Col. 3:12–14).

How might we reflect deeply and grow in self-awareness of our character? We can begin with prayer and go to the one who searches and knows us fully as David did in Psalm 139. Meditate and pray, "Search me, O God, and know my heart! Try me and know my thoughts! And see if there be any grievous way in me, and lead me in the way everlasting" (Ps. 139:23–24).

We also can grow in self-awareness of our character by intentionally asking two or three people who know you well to soberly and candidly describe their experience of your personhood and leadership. Ask them, "How do you experience me?"

Finally, make it a practice to ask those you counsel for feedback.

"Your reflection on how I give counsel helps me to grow. How was my counsel helpful or unhelpful to you?" When I pose this question to church parishioners, they often respond with gratitude only, so then I follow up with, "How could my counsel have been *more* helpful to you?" Although it might be challenging to ask for honest feedback in an honor–shame culture, church leaders humble enough to ask for feedback set an important example.

Build Strong Relationships

Beyond the character of the pastor or leader providing counsel, building genuine relationships is also crucial. When redemptive relationships are deliberately fostered, healthy change happens. Intriguingly, a study comparing the effectiveness of various counseling treatment approaches showed that all the various approaches (cognitive behavioral, interpersonal, etc.) comparatively, had similar effectiveness related to outcomes and positive change. This research identified a robust relationship between the therapeutic alliance (the bond between the counselor and the client) and treatment outcome across a broad spectrum of treatments in a variety of client problem contexts. These studies concluded that diverse counseling approaches provide similar beneficial effects to counselees.[14] Further studies found that the strength of the relationship is the most potent contributor to the outcome for various presenting issues.[15]

How might you intentionally build this strong relationship of trust and safety? It begins with faith that our God who began a good work in his children will "bring it to completion at the day of Jesus Christ" (Phil. 1:6). God gives the growth. Another important way to strengthen the relationship is to join the person in their struggle. At the outset of your counseling conversation, ask: "As we join together and talk, tell me about what you hope for? What do you believe we need to figure out together?"

Know Your People

Last, Asian American church leaders can provide better counsel by tailoring their preaching or home group studies to address common ills or suffering—things like depression, anxiety, loss, and difficult family dynamics. This provides intentional guidance, genuine compassion, and gospel hope in an honoring way.

The concept of counseling is not absent in Asian culture, but the modern practice of seeing a professional counselor still meets strong headwinds. Yet, Asian immigrant–American churches can still be effective in counseling those in need.

Future Directions

Factors such as acculturation, the decreasing stigma of seeking mental health/counseling help, and a growing awareness of issues related to mental illness and suffering continue to provide the church with opportunities to counsel those in need. The Asian American church finds itself at a critical juncture. Historically, we've been limited in our role to provide organized counseling to the people of God because of cultural factors like honor and shame dynamics. Yet, even that limited counsel was beneficial, and the more it increases, the healthier the church will become. Asian American church leaders can learn from our history and serve the emerging generations through Christian counseling and psychology for the sake of our people and the glory of Christ.

5

Bridging the Gap: The Key to Thriving
in Immigrant Ministry

by Michael Lee

We all know what it's like to be asked a question masquerading as a statement. Ten years ago, when I told my friends I had accepted a call to serve in the English ministry of a Korean immigrant church, I often heard questions like, "So you're going back into the Korean church?" "Have you considered working for a non-Korean church?" "Is your wife on board with this?" (Korean churches are notorious for burdening a pastor's wife.) It was evident my decision surprised many and disappointed others. I was leaving an independent, Asian American church to serve in an English ministry half our size, with half our budget, existing in the shadow of a Korean megachurch.

I was keenly aware of the trending ministry landscape in Southern California where I live. A growing number of independent Asian American ministries were flourishing, while many tethered to an immigrant church were struggling. Many Asian Americans were planting churches while others were stepping into visible leadership roles at majority-culture churches. Anyone serving as an English ministry pastor felt left behind in a ministry model that was regarded as outdated and undesirable. If you had options, you got out. No one I knew was going back in.

To be clear, I don't believe every Asian American pastor is wired or called to work alongside an immigrant church. I love the many ways that God is using Asian American leaders for his kingdom. However, there's still a significant need for English-speaking Asian Americans to minister alongside immigrant congregations. And I absolutely believe we can flourish in this space. Present and future generations of Asian American Christians are counting on us to figure this out.

Reentry

When I returned to an immigrant church, no one was more surprised than me! As I considered a ministry transition, I skipped over every job post that said, "English Ministry Pastor." As a pastor in my thirties, I was looking for a step forward and a step up. A Korean church felt like a step back.

However, over the course of my search, a job post appeared in my inbox and caught my eye: "English Ministry Pastor of All Nations Church." If the name of the church had been any different, I would have ignored it. But I had spoken at a couple of their retreats and knew some of the people. The church was well-regarded, and the Korean senior pastor was a respected leader. My curiosity was piqued. What if God had valuable ministry lessons in store for me?

In addition to the unattractive idea of working at a Korean church again, there was another big drawback: this church was located in the valley. For those unfamiliar with Southern California, the valley is not where most people want to be. Downtown is dynamic and relevant. Orange County is the mecca. The valley was considered a place where English ministries struggled, and pastors didn't last.

But as I pondered this opportunity, God laid two questions on my heart. First, was I willing to serve in an underserved area? Second, did I believe God was calling me to serve Asian Americans? As I reflected and prayed through these two questions, the answer was yes. Psalm 78 describes a call to declare the works of the Lord from generation to generation: "We will not hide them from their children, but tell to the coming generation the glorious deeds of the LORD, and his might, and the wonders that he has done" (Ps. 78:4). When I read this, my heart gravitated toward the community I could serve at All Nations. As an Asian American, I carried a burden for the next generation of my community to know Christ. I believed it was part of God's plan to reach the nations—and all people groups—for his glory. With these two convictions in my heart—to serve the underserved and help the Korean American church—I accepted the position.

The Importance of Self-Awareness

As I write this chapter, I'm beginning my tenth year at All Nations Community Church. Today we are a fully particularized congregation with our own membership, officers, staff, and governance. We exist in an interdependent model alongside the Korean ministry and over the years, God has been truly kind and gracious to us. At the same time, I'm painfully aware this has *not* been the experience for many English ministries in Korean churches. Statistics and stories remind me that what we enjoy at All Nations is exceptional.

How did we get here? What best practices help it work? I wholeheartedly believe a clear system and structure is important, but I'm convinced the most important work is *in you*. You must become the kind of leader who can understand and navigate the challenges of this ministry context. Become the kind of leader who can manage change with patience and diplomacy. In my experience, no system or model can save unhealthy leaders from themselves. No one talks themselves out of quitting by looking at bylaws, organizational charts, or even a vision statement. It's only because the Lord has continually developed my character that I've been able to remain in ministry alongside an immigrant church. This can be your story too.

One of the most helpful resources on this topic is a collection of articles titled, "On Emotional Intelligence" published by the *Harvard Business Review*. In the first article, Daniel Goleman defines self-awareness as "knowing one's strengths, weaknesses, drives, values, and impact on others."[16] That last phrase was incredibly helpful for me. Self-awareness is not simply a matter of understanding my own emotions and abilities. It is also a matter of understanding my impact on others—in other words, how people experience me.

Have you ever considered how people experience you? Not what people *think* about you but how they *experience* you. What is it like to be around you when you're stressed, tired, or frustrated? What is it like to be in a conversation or meeting with you? What is it like when people receive feedback from you or try to offer feedback to you? Many leaders never deeply consider this.

The Skill of Diplomacy

Considering how others experience us is an immense tool for cross-cultural ministry. Asian culture is deeply rooted in the consideration of others. This is why we often have a hard time telling people no. This is why so much communication for Asians is nonverbal. Many in the first generation want to be considered and understood without having to spell things out. Obviously, this can lead to a lot of confusion, frustration, and judgment from people with different values. To help us navigate this at All Nations, I've chosen diplomacy as *the* skill we strive to embody.

I define diplomacy as "the skill of bringing diverse people together in order to make progress." How do we bring different groups of people with different values and objectives together? How do we avoid putting things off and prevent leadership discussions from ending in stalemates? The answer is diplomacy.

This may feel confusing to many Korean Americans. Why would we need diplomacy to speak to our own children or parents? It's because a significant cultural gap exists between first- and second-generation Korean Americans. Years ago, a mentor reminded me that just as missionaries are careful not to impose their own cultural norms on other people groups, we must exhibit the same degree of mindfulness with the first generation. I never thought of my parents as a different people group from me, but in many ways they are. So many of our frustrations with the first-generation church stem from assuming a shared culture when in reality, we are different. We have different approaches when it comes to making decisions, creating ministry budgets, communicating events, and shepherding our people. A diplomacy mindset helps us move from judgment and criticism to understanding and cooperation.

Diplomacy doesn't mean I always take it on the chin or defer to the oldest person in the room. There are times when I've had to decline requests or advocate for facility usage on our campus. I've had difficult conversations with staff members from the Korean ministry to address complaints and conflicts. But just as diplomats navigate geopolitical issues with extreme caution, I am exceedingly careful in my interactions with the Korean church.

Practicing diplomacy with the immigrant church is not simply a matter of being courteous. It also means you must put in the effort to show you care. Whenever I have the opportunity, I participate in the life of the Korean church. I make myself available to help and contribute. We give our time, our money, and ourselves to the Korean ministry. I celebrate and affirm what the Lord is doing in their church. I try to communicate that their welfare is as important to us as ours is to them. As a result, God has blessed us with ten rich years of peace and unity. We've completed two facility renovations and are planning a future building project together. This would not be possible without a deep sense of mutual trust and respect, which has grown from the seeds of consistent diplomacy.

Navigating Change

Although I won't unpack our model of interdependence here, I will share how it came about. For those interested in learning about different models of ministries with Asian American churches, I recommend *Tapestry of Grace* by Benjamin C. Shin and Sheryl Silzer.[17] It's often said that people don't fear change; they fear loss. That is absolutely true when it comes to the mindset of the first-generation Korean church. Their greatest fear is to see an English ministry grow and thrive, only to break off as an independent church later. They've heard stories of it happening all over America and perhaps even experienced it firsthand.

When I began my time at All Nations, we were a department under the umbrella of the Korean church. I like to think of this time as a season of incubation. We were protected and provided for by our mother church. We were able to do ministry without any financial obligations or burdens. Our only expectation was to help the Korean church minister to the younger generation and do our best to retain college students and young adults.

As our ministry grew and matured, we sensed a need to particularize. It became increasingly difficult to establish membership and church governance without becoming independent. For example, what did it mean for our members to belong to the Korean church as confessing members? How would our elders and deacons be approved by both congregations, and how would they lead and govern in the church? Because we could not answer these questions with clarity and conviction, we began conversations about becoming independent.

Now, remembering the fears of the first-generation church, we used the metaphor of family to help them understand our vision and motivation. I asked the elders: What is your vision for your children? What kinds of things do you want for them when they become adults? In addition to following Jesus, they envisioned that their children would graduate from school, get jobs, get married and start families, purchase homes, and so on. Their vision for their children was to become fully fledged adults who were still connected to family. I told our elders, "This is what we are becoming, and this is what we want as well. We will always be your children. We're just now your adult children." And they understood. They unanimously approved, and today, our motto for interdependence is: "One Family, Two Churches, with One Great Commission."

What would it look like if the first and second generations embraced the metaphor of the church as family? What if being seen as the children of the first generation isn't a bad thing? Perhaps we just never stuck around long enough to enter adulthood and enjoy it together.

I would be amiss if I didn't share that the relationship between both lead pastors is critical. I recently encouraged an English ministry looking for a new lead pastor to actively include the senior pastor of the Korean church in their search process. Personally, I'm beyond indebted to Reverend Jinsoo Yoo and Reverend Tae Kim, who were both my senior pastors while serving at All Nations. These men carried a vision to support and empower the second-generation church. They were willing to take risks, make space, and advocate for our ministry. English ministries cannot flourish without the shared vision of the senior pastor, so I recommend that you spend as much time as possible with them. You will never be fully empowered to lead your ministry without the trust of the senior pastor. So whatever it takes, invest in that relationship because you will not be able to flourish without it.

To everyone in the trenches of ministry alongside the immigrant church or considering reentry, may we remember Paul's words to the Philippians, "Convinced of this, I know that I will remain and continue with you all, for your progress and joy in the faith, so that in me you may have ample cause to glory in Christ Jesus" (Phil. 1:25–26). I can't imagine where my generation would be without the sacrifices and efforts of the first-generation church. I pray that they won't have to envision their future without us.

PART II

THE ASIAN AMERICAN CHURCH

6

Rediscovering Joy: How I Learned to Love the Asian American Church

by Owen Y. Lee

In the late 1990s and early 2000s, there was a concerted push for Asian American pastors to lead their predominantly Asian American churches to become more multiethnic or to start planting multiethnic churches. The driving conviction was that the biblical vision was for churches to be multiethnic, especially in "multiethnic America."

Revelation 7:9–17 was typically cited as the biblical basis for pursuing this vision. The logic went like this: Since the demographic makeup of heaven will be multiethnic (redeemed people from every nation, tribe, and tongue), and since the local church is supposed to be a colony of heaven (that represents and reflects heaven), every church should strive to be multiethnic.

This logic seemed sound, and the vision was beautiful and compelling. I was sold. I earnestly desired to pastor a multiethnic church, because I began to believe the multiethnic church was more biblical than the monoethnic church.

At the time, I pastored a Korean American church in Southern California. I began to lose hope our church would ever become more than "just" a Korean American church, given its close ties with a first-generation, immigrant, Korean-speaking church. Even though I was ministering to second-generation, English-speaking Korean Americans, the church began to look, sound, feel, and even smell "too ethnically Korean" for my liking. It was hard for me to imagine non-Asian people joining and flourishing in our church. To me, our lack of ethnic diversity felt unbiblical.

And so, to realize my dream of pastoring a multiethnic church, I sought the permission and blessing of our Korean American church to plant a new church. I even transferred my membership from a Korean-language presbytery to an Anglo presbytery so everyone would know we were seeking to plant a racially and ethnically diverse church, *not* an Asian American church. To me, being a multiethnic church essentially meant having fewer Asian American people and more White people. In my mind, this would make our church not only more multiethnic but also more legitimate.

Although our core planting group consisted of only Asian Americans, I was naively hopeful non-Asians would show up and join our church. No longer limited by our ties to a first-generation, Korean-speaking immigrant church, surely this was possible, right?

To my surprise and disappointment, most of the people who visited and stayed at our church were Asian Americans. There were *some* non-Asians who visited our church, but few stayed. Our church did have some non-Asians who integrated, but it was obvious we were a majority Asian American church.

Secretly, I struggled with that, and it led to some sinful thoughts and actions. When Asian Americans visited, I would resent their presence—because they were making an already Asian American church look and feel even more Asian. Ultimately, they were getting in the way of my dream. When non-Asians visited, I was elated—they could help fulfill my dream. My partiality for non-Asians over Asians was completely sinful and unloving.

No matter how much we tried to downplay and even mute our ethnicity and culture, and no matter how welcoming and how inclusive we tried to be, after many years, we were still a majority Asian American church. I wrestled with questions like, "What is wrong with our church that non-Asians rarely stay and integrate? What is wrong with me that non-Asians do not want me as their pastor?"

Although I didn't know how to articulate it at the time, I was ashamed of our church—it had failed to become a "biblical" multiethnic church. And I envied other Asian American pastors who were successfully leading multiethnic congregations. I felt inferior and lacking. When asked about the demographic makeup of my church at pastors' conferences and gatherings, I'd respond with a note of embarrassment, "Oh, we're *just* a Korean American church."

The vision of the multiethnic church, which was once so beautiful to me, became burdensome. It kept me from fully loving the church God entrusted to me. You can't truly love a church when you secretly resent it for not being the kind of church that you wanted. I idolized the vision of the multiethnic church more than I had loved the actual Asian American church that Jesus gave me to love and serve.

Over time, by the grace of God, I came to realize that Jesus valued our predominantly Asian American church, *as it was*. We didn't have to become more multiethnic for Jesus to love us more. And that's when everything changed for me. I began to love, with joy and without apology, my Asian American church.

What transformed my understanding of the Asian American church? A large part of it was Scripture. Ironically, while I thought the only way to be biblical was to cultivate a multiethnic church, I discovered that Scripture's view of the church is even bigger than I imagined.

A Glorious Future

The vision of Revelation 7:9–17 tells us that the kingdom of heaven, when it fully comes, will be beautifully and gloriously pan-ethnic (all nations), not just multiethnic (many nations). There will be redeemed image bearers from every race, nation, ethnicity, tribe, and language! They will be dressed in robes made white by the blood of the Lamb, and they will stand before the throne and before the Lamb, crying out, "Salvation belongs to our God, who sits on the throne, and to the Lamb." And they will dwell with the Shepherd Lamb in that place where sin, suffering, tears, and death will be no more. This glorious future awaits us, when the risen and reigning Lord Jesus returns to establish the new heaven and new earth.

The beautiful and glorious pan-ethnicity of the kingdom of heaven is partially reflected in the church today. And it's reflected in the *global* church—*not in any single local church.* Every local church around the world—from every nation, state, city, suburb, town, and village—partially reflects the racial and ethnic diversity that will be gloriously present in the everlasting kingdom of heaven.

Until the fullness of God's kingdom comes, there will be different types of churches—monoethnic and multiethnic—scattered throughout the world. In America, where people from different racial, ethnic, and cultural heritages live together, there will be different types of churches: majority White churches, majority Black churches, majority Brown churches, majority Asian churches, and multiethnic churches, just to name a few. Each one is good, beautiful, and legitimate, and *collectively*, they reflect the fullness of the kingdom of God. No one local church is big enough or diverse enough to do that.

The Bible acknowledges and celebrates different types of churches. In the New Testament, we see majority Jewish churches (the church in Jerusalem), majority gentile churches (the churches in Philippi and Galatia), and mixed churches that had both Jews and gentiles (the church in Rome). Every church—whether monoethnic or multiethnic—has strengths and weaknesses, opportunities, and challenges. One kind of church is not more biblical or superior to another. Every church that belongs to King Jesus is equally beautiful and precious to Him, and they are all useful for advancing his kingdom in different ways in different places and among different peoples.

In God's providence, some churches are more multiethnic than others. However, most churches in the world, and throughout history, have been largely monoethnic, even in America. The vision of the multiethnic church is a heavy burden when forced upon local churches. However, the vision is partially fulfilled in the *global* church, and it's beautiful! The well-intentioned call for every local church to become multiethnic is misguided, unbiblical, and burdensome. Because Jesus loves and celebrates *all* his churches, so should we. And because Jesus loves and celebrates the Asian American church, so should we.

Strengths of the Asian American Church

Every church (no matter its ethnic makeup and location in the world) contributes to God's kingdom. Although not exhaustive, here are four key contributions that Asian American churches can make to the global church.

A Place That's Home

Asian American Christians live in a liminal space, struggling to feel at home in any space. As an Asian American Christian, I often feel like a minority in someone else's majority culture. I have always longed to belong—not just as a welcomed guest in someone else's home—but in a home of my own, with a family of my own.

Growing up in America, I was a minority in a majority White culture. From Monday to Friday, whether at school or at work, I was a minority. But as a second-generation, English-speaking Korean Christian, I was also a minority at church, where most members (and those in power) were first-generation, Korean-speaking Christians. In every space, I had to code-switch to fit in with whatever majority culture I found myself in. It was, and still is, exhausting. None of those spaces felt like home.

The church where I currently serve as pastor is a Korean American, English-speaking church. Many of our members have told me, "Pastor Owen, for the first time in my life, I finally feel like I'm at home." Why do they feel that way? Because for the first time they get to be part of majority culture! For most of their lives, they have been minorities in someone else's majority culture. For the first time, they are culturally comfortable, feel seen and understood by others who share their experiences, and are free to be their authentic and unedited selves. And they don't have to code-switch.

For the first time, the majority of the people in the church not only look like them and believe like them, but also share in their experience of living as Asians in America. They don't stick out, yet they feel more seen than ever before. They are in a church full of Korean Americans who love Korean food and culture but struggle to speak Korean. They are in a church where the people in senior leadership look like them. Those who determine the vision, mission, values, and culture of the church—they look and think like them. For the first time, they believe they can lay down roots for the long haul and raise their families in this church. Maybe they would struggle to serve in any significant leadership capacity at a Korean-speaking church or a White church, but they can imagine themselves serving here.

Our church is a regional commuter church. Some people drive over thirty-five miles, past dozens of other churches, to get here. Many of those churches have better facilities, better preaching, better worship, and better everything else. So why commute all the way to Centreville to be a part of our church? To feel at home.

As Christians, we are exiles and sojourners in this world. Heaven is our true home. Until we get there, the church is supposed to be our home away from home. A pastor friend of mine put it this way: "When church doesn't feel like home, we feel doubly exiled."

Contextualized Discipleship

The Asian American church is well-positioned to address pastoral challenges and discipleship issues facing Asian American Christians.

For example, during COVID, the sudden and dramatic rise of anti-Asian racism and violence, especially against the elderly and women, was alarming and disorienting. Many Asian American Christians were traumatized and turned to their Asian American churches to process their pain and confusion. It was a refuge where they received pastoral care and biblical encouragement.

After the mass shooting in a Korean spa in Atlanta in March 2021, many Asian Americans were angry, afraid, and confused. My teenage son asked me, "Dad, why (are) they killing us?" With so many hurting people in our church, we hosted a Night of Lament via Zoom. We came together to share our feelings, fears, anxieties, sadness, rage, and confusion. It was a space for Asian American Christians to be honest and raw about our emotions. We read Scripture together, affirmed the dignity and value of Asian American lives, justly condemned anti-Asian racism and hatred, and prayed. We had the opportunity to minister to grieving Asian Americans, helping them lament and cling to the hope of the gospel.

Asian American churches also have the opportunity to affirm the dignity, worth, and beauty of Asian Americans as image bearers. Because of White cultural normativity, we sometimes experience the subtle shame of not measuring up to White standards of beauty. I once preached a sermon where one of the points of application was to affirm the beauty of Asian features. I said, "Yes, blond hair and big blue eyes are beautiful. *But so are black hair and small brown eyes!* Asian skin color and facial features are just as beautiful!" Afterward, several sisters shared how healing it was for them to hear this from the pulpit, and they expressed deep gratitude that this truth was affirmed publicly.

Developing Asian American Leaders

In the church where I serve as pastor, nearly all the staff, officers, and lay leaders are Asian Americans. Some of these gifted leaders would probably not be invited into leadership positions in a non-Asian American church, because their gifts may be overlooked or unappreciated in those contexts. Many majority White churches and multiethnic churches tend to view Asian American pastors as wonderful assistants or associate pastors, but not as senior pastor material. The Asian American church has the opportunity and responsibility to recognize and raise up such leaders into senior roles.

Unique Gospel Opportunities

I live now in Northern Virginia, where lots of dechurched and unchurched Asian Americans are unlikely to visit a majority White or multiethnic church. But they might be open to visiting an Asian American church.

Our church, along with other Asian American churches in Northern Virginia, reaches dechurched and unchurched Asian Americans in ways that most non-Asian churches simply cannot. One church is inherently more effective than another church at reaching a certain demographic in their region, and no church can effectively reach everyone in their area. In general, Asian American churches tend to be more effective and fruitful at reaching Asian Americans than non-Asian churches are. Yes, there are certainly exceptions. But, by and large, Asian American churches have seen greater fruitfulness in their ministry among Asian Americans than among non-Asians. This does *not* mean Asian American churches should focus exclusively on reaching Asian Americans with the gospel. But a humble recognition that different churches are fruitful and effective at reaching different kinds of people should lead churches to an awareness of their need of partnership and collaboration. Rather than compete against each another, we can collaborate to reach more people in our regions with the gospel.

Treasure and Celebrate Your Church!

Every Sunday, when I stand up to preach the gospel to my Asian American church, I think to myself, "This church is beautiful and precious to Jesus *just as they are.* They don't have to become more ethnically diverse for Jesus to love them more or for me to love them more. They are beautiful, precious, and cherished by their Savior—

just as they are."

By the grace of God, I have been liberated from the burden of the vision of the multiethnic church. Now, I don't just *tolerate* my Asian American church—I *celebrate* it! And I love and celebrate my Asian American church because Jesus does. I hope and pray that you would too, because Jesus does!

7

Hopeful Exiles: A Theology of the
Asian American Experience

by Aaron J. Chung

In 2019, our urban church had a fall retreat in the quaint town of Princeton, New Jersey. Because we were located just a few blocks from Times Square, our church looked forward to exchanging the concrete jungle of New York City for the beautiful foliage of Princeton every year. Our church's name is Exilic, but when we arrived at our hotel, the concierge handed me a large manila envelope labeled "Exotic Presbyterian Church." I laughed! Oxymorons like "jumbo shrimp" are one thing, but pairing *exotic* and *presbyterian* is quite another.

We named our church *Exilic* as a reminder that this world is not our home. The nagging feeling many Asian American Christians experience—that we don't belong—is part of following Jesus. However, beyond the usual feelings of displacement common to all disciples, Asian Americans live with an intensified, multilayered sense of unbelonging. This may sound discouraging, but by diving deeper into the theology of exile, we can live more purposefully and peacefully, knowing we are not the first ones to experience it. There are three reasons why exile should be a major theme in Asian American theology:

1. Exile is a major theme for God's people in Scripture.
2. Exile is a major theme in Asian American life.
3. Understanding exile helps us faithfully move forward.

Exile in Scripture

Exile describes the condition of living away from one's home. This doesn't mean spending a semester abroad or doing missionary work overseas, however. Exile means you are kicked out of your home; in ancient times, exile not only meant banishment but also death. This theme of exile is pervasive on almost every page of Scripture from Genesis to Revelation. Since the fall of man in Genesis 3, the human experience has been one of exile. Genesis 3:23–24 says, "the LORD God *sent him out* from the garden of Eden.... He drove out the man, and at the *east of the garden of Eden* he placed the cherubim and a flaming sword..." When God sent Adam and Eve out of Eden, he exiled them. As a result, the world is now filled with sickness, natural disasters, pandemics, broken systems, injustice, racism, abuse, and of course, the stench of death.

And yet, the story of Scripture is also infused with hope. God's people are not permanent travelers aimlessly wandering and never arriving, but we are pilgrims on a journey back home. As the ever so wise Gandalf says, "Not all those who wander are lost."[18] As followers of Jesus, you and I aren't perpetual exiles because our ultimate citizenship is in heaven. Until that glorious day, we advance through life as exiles, which is why John Bunyan referred to the Christian life as *The Pilgrim's Progress.*[19]

For example, in the Old Testament, Abraham wandered as a vagabond; Moses and the Israelites were nomads in the wilderness; Esther, Daniel, and Ezekiel endured exile to Assyria or Babylon; and Jeremiah was taken to Egypt against his will. Similarly, in the New Testament, Christians are called *aliens, strangers, sojourners,* and *exiles* (e.g., see 1 Peter 1:1, 2:11; Eph. 2:19; Heb. 11:13). And of course, Jesus was the ultimate exile, who willingly left heaven for earth.

Most exiles are involuntary, yet Jesus willingly exiled himself to be our "Immanuel ... God with us" (Matt. 1:23). If you put John 3:16 in the framework of exile, it reads, "For God so loved the world that he [*exiled*] his one and only Son." The only way for us to reenter Eden is for someone to be exiled in our place. On our own we could never barge through the flaming swords guarding Eden, but because Jesus was slain under those flaming swords of judgment (via a cross), we who were exiled can now come back home.

Exile as the Asian American Experience

Whether you know it or not, as an Asian American, the theme of exile has been your experience your whole life. For most second-generation Asian Americans, we had no say when it came to our relocation here. And for better and worse, it changed us. My family moved to the United States when I was two years old, but despite living in America for over forty years now, I still feel out of place—like a square peg trying to fit into a round hole. At the same time, whenever I go back to Korea, I know I don't fully belong there either. I can't speak Korean, and I'm culturally too American. So where do I fit? The truth is, I don't fit. Biblically speaking, however, am I supposed to? While the Asian American church can create a tangible sense of belonging (which is good), ultimately, as exilic Christians, we still feel misplaced because we aren't home yet.

After G. K. Chesterton became a follower of Jesus, he said, "I knew now … why I could feel homesick at home."[20] Have you ever felt this way? For many Asian Americans, feeling homesick at home has been our perpetual experience. Yet, home is the very thing we've yearned for our entire lives. Lee Isaac Chung, the director of the award-winning film, *Minari*, says, "Of all texts, Scripture was most likely the biggest reference for the script. The Bible includes many stories about gardens and farming, and the entire arc of its narrative seems to place key moments of betrayal and redemption within gardens. *Minari* is a story of immigrants, but at its heart, it's about a family trying to find a new life. They've left one garden and are in search of another."[21]

As exiles, we long for home. For Eden. This longing is especially true for Asian Americans, but it wasn't something that I initially noticed.

When we first named our church "Exilic," we knew it related to the Christian life but didn't think about its relevance for Asian Americans. My identity was built upon White adjacency and assimilation, which produced a truncated view of what it meant to be an Asian American Christian. This blinded me from seeing the Word of God through an Asian American Christian lens.

A few years ago, scholar Esau McCaulley wrote a book titled, *Reading While Black*, which emphasizes the role of interpreting Scripture through the lens of the African American experience.[22] For me, I was *Reading While Wanting to be White*, which is why most of my library was written by White theologians. I didn't realize Asian Americans can see things non-Asians can't, which is why I began to wonder: What does reading while Asian look like? And what could it potentially contribute to the larger body of Christ?

The Black community has contributed so much to the body of Christ. Musically, they've given us blues, jazz, and gospel music. Generally speaking, White preaching tends to emphasize three points in a sermon, and Black preaching tends to emphasize one major point, which is more effective and memorable from an oratory perspective. Black theology is also justice-oriented with a deep concern for the poor and marginalized. The body of Christ would be anemic without the contributions of our Black brothers and sisters.

But what exactly is Asian American theology? If Black theology is compatible with an orthodox theology of liberation, Asian American theology is compatible with a theology of exile. For example, when I read about how the major prophets speak about the Israelite deportation to Babylon and how they moved from the majority to the minority, I empathize with that as an immigrant who moved to America. When Daniel was given his Babylonian name, Belteshazzar, to fit into his new culture better, I relate as someone who was given a name to fit into my new culture better as well. When Daniel had to learn a new second language, I resonate because English is my second language. No one's story is identical, but this exilic theme resonates undeniably to the Asian American experience.

I moved to America when I was two but didn't receive my US citizenship until I was twenty-two. So, for twenty years I was a *resident alien*, someone caught between two worlds. Hebrews 11:13–14 alludes to this when it says, "These all died in faith, not having received the things promised, but having seen them and greeted them from afar, and having acknowledged that they were *strangers* and *exiles* on the earth. For people who speak thus make it clear that they are seeking a *homeland*" (emphasis added).

In this same chapter of Hebrews, the author reminds us how

Abraham was from the land of Ur, then moved to Canaan, but his ultimate citizenship was in heaven. Just like you, Abraham lived a hyphenated life. As an Ur-Canaanite whose citizenship was in heaven, Abraham didn't quite fit in anywhere. Asian Americans understand this because we've lived hyphenated lives as Chinese Americans, Japanese Americans, Korean Americans, and so forth. This hyphenated life has positive and negative aspects to it.

Positively, Asian Americans know all too well that America is not our ultimate home. When constantly asked the question, "Where are you from?," how can we possibly feel at home? Yet, this perpetual sense of limbo is a blessing in disguise, because when you constantly feel at home, it becomes much harder to long for your eternal home. When Babylon becomes your Eden, the American dream becomes your only dream. If we, as Asian Americans, steward our displaced experiences well by sharing our stories (much like this book), we have an exilic mindset to offer the greater body of Christ.

Negatively, our hyphenated life means that as Asian Americans we often feel like the narrator in Ralph Ellison's *Invisible Man*.[23] We feel overlooked, unseen, and ignored in meetings and conversations. Sadly, this happens even within the body of Christ. The race conversation is a Black and White binary not only in our culture but also in the church. Far too often, we are not the right kind of minority the majority culture wants. Even in multiethnic churches that supposedly value diversity, the most gifted Asian American friends are offered the assistant pastor role, but not the senior pastor role. In seminary, I never had one Asian or Asian American author on my syllabus. As Jay Kaspian Kang writes, we often feel like the "loneliest Americans."[24] If studies about our current epidemic of loneliness are true, this feeling of loneliness is especially brutalizing for Asian Americans.

Many lonely Americans have found a home in the Asian American church. The actor, Steven Yeun, once said, "Sometimes I wonder if the Asian American experience is what it's like when you're thinking about everyone else, but nobody else is thinking about you."[25] Can you relate? If Yeun is right, the Asian American church must continually be a place where people are seen and valued—where they can finally be their true and unapologetic selves. Until we experience our true home, this sense of belonging—even in shadow form—is a gift the Asian American church can offer.

The Way Forward in Exile

Prior to George Floyd's tragic death, one of the chief complaints about Exilic was that it was too Asian. After this tragedy, however, this rhetoric faded significantly. In fact, I haven't heard a single complaint about our church being too Asian since 2020. If anything, I have seen more Asian Americans flock to our church precisely because of our demographic. We used to be the church you had to apologetically invite your non-Asian friends to, but today that insecure self-hatred is completely gone.

As someone who's lived all over the world, finding a home away from home has helped me adjust to new environments. The Asian American church has an opportunity to be a safe haven for those who feel displaced—a space where people are seen, known, and loved. This requires more than telling inside jokes, talking about K-dramas, and eating Chinese takeout in community groups. We've already done this, and it hasn't helped with our identity crisis or our lack of contribution to the *greater* body of Christ. A true home is where we can be our true selves, but it's also a place where we can have difficult living room conversations about who we are and what we are called to do.

We must provide a space to discuss the intersection of our faith and identity as Asian American Christians, whether hosting panels on Asian American Pacific Islander (AAPI) hate, preaching about our identity through an Asian American Christian lens, discussing how the gospel impacts an honor–shame culture, navigating the tensions between the Korean and the Black communities, lamenting spiritual abuse, or talking about how we can steward our White adjacency to help other minorities.

Without a church to call home, we risk feeling doubly exiled because we're already away from our heavenly home. The church must be a life-giving oasis for Asian Americans within this Babylonian moment. A theology of exile is critical for the Asian American church to embrace if we are going to thrive this side of heaven.

I recognize that the next generation of Asian Americans might feel more at home in America than previous generations. My kids certainly do. However, our experience of exile isn't going away any time soon, so there will be a lot of overlap. The next generation will have their own stories to tell, but they will not be able to tell their stories unless we give them shoulders to stand on.

Right now, Asian food, dramas, and music are influencing the world. I love seeing kimchi and soup dumplings finally being sold at Trader Joes and Costco. It's about time! I love the fact that people of all colors are singing BTS. I love that *Squid Game* has shattered records on Netflix. I love that Simu Liu is the main hero in *Shang-Chi*. But I also dream of a day when Asian American Christianity is influencing the greater body of Christ as much as our food, dramas, and music. I yearn for a day when the blind spots within the greater body of Christ slowly disappear and we become spiritually richer because of it. We have something to offer. *You* have something to offer.

The Japanese theologian, Kosuke Koyama, pictures a group of exiles standing before the pearly gates after a long and arduous journey called *life*. Tired and weary, barely able to stand on their dusty feet, Koyama imagines Jesus opening the gates and saying to these exhausted sojourners, "You've had a difficult journey. You must be tired, and dirty. Let me wash your feet. The banquet is ready."[26] As exiles, this is the future that awaits us, but until that glorious day when we arrive home, we journey with something great to offer the entire body of Christ—an exilic mindset.

8

Exegete Your People: Understanding the Heartbeat of Asian American Congregations

by Steve S. Chang

During college I attended a large church with a pastor known for his expository preaching. My friends and I made the thirty-minute drive with our NASB Study Bibles, pens, and sermon notes in hand, eager to learn. I purchased sermon tapes to listen to messages I missed and relistened to sermons for greater clarity. Desiring to grow more, I enrolled in a seminary whose mission was to produce pastors who would "preach the Word." I still believe a commitment to the unchanging, inerrant Word of God is central to any ministry; yet, through the years I've learned another dimension to pastoring.

In seminary, a professor challenged us to exegete not only the Bible but also our people. Ministry cannot simply be about the pastor and the Bible—it must be about the pastor and the Bible and the people. We need to know our sheep.

As evangelical Asian American pastors steeped in majority-culture professors, books, media, brands, and voices, we unknowingly mimic ministry designed for the majority context instead of stewarding our own. But the pains and idols of Asian Americans require a more contextual approach to discipleship, care, and church. Without it, the church risks losing the emerging generation of Asian Americans. So, whether your context is an immigrant church, a third-culture Asian American church, or even a multiethnic church, you must know your people.

Knowing Asian Americans

Who are Asian Americans? It's impossible to generalize, but here are a few characteristics that are true of many who identify as English-speaking Asian Americans.

Spiritually Rootless

Because most Asians immigrated to the United States after 1968, the children of first-generation immigrants are relatively young and do not have deep generational or cultural roots in the United States. Most lack the geographical history, generational wealth, institutional power, or social connections often associated with being a part of a community through generations.

Spiritually, they tend to be nomads, not tethered generationally to one church or tradition. A typical second-generation Asian American story goes as follows. She grows up in her parents' immigrant church and enjoys youth group. If her faith survives the adolescence stage, she says goodbye to the immigrant church upon entering college and explores faith through a parachurch ministry on campus or a non-immigrant church near campus. If her faith survives college, she moves to the city for work and finds a church that provides an environment and community for those on a similar journey. She pursues the American dream in her career, marriage, family, and a home in the suburbs with a good school district. If her faith survives the pursuit of the

American dream, she looks for a church her kids will love. If her faith survives all these life stages, she has now cycled through four churches. If she still has faith, her faith may lack the deep rootedness that comes from being tethered to a faith tradition. Without that long-term faith community, the child of the immigrant generation can adopt a Christianity that is rootless, untethered, and unguided.

Culturally Dissonant

In addition, many Asian Americans live in a culturally dissonant reality, in which they have to navigate two cultures. This is exhausting and disorienting.

The first-generation immigrant's language and culture is inevitably tied to their country of origin, including various religious, historical, and political influences. Compared to those who grew up in the States, their worldview is more likely to be hierarchical (rather than egalitarian), communal (rather than individualistic), dutiful (rather than emotional), and works-oriented (rather than rights-oriented).

The second generation must navigate two cultures: the culture of their parents and the culture of the majority. A second-generation son must constantly code-switch from home, school, work, and social settings. He visits the home of a White friend who tells him to feel at home. He is conflicted because feeling "at home" means taking his shoes off when that is not the practice in his friend's home. What does it mean to be home? As bicultural and bilingual (for many), he feels out of place in both settings.

Racially Marginal

Many of us in the second generation believed that mastery of the English language, a high income, a house in the suburbs, and separation from the immigrant generation would make us authentic Americans. But as we grew older, an invisible barrier still kept us from being seen as Americans.

Mia Tuan, in *Forever Foreigners or Honorary Whites? The Asian Ethnic Experience Today*, gives the results of her interviews of middle-class, third-generation Chinese and Japanese Americans about their ethnic identities and concluded that Asian Americans: (1) exercise flexibility in the cultural elements they choose to retain or discard; (2) feel external pressures to identify themselves ethnically and racially as such; (3) are assumed to be foreign despite generational longevity; and (4) are not considered "real" Americans.[27] Even in 2023, 78 percent of Asian adults experience incidents that made them feel as if they were forever foreigners.[28] Dr. Sharon Kim concludes, "No matter how hard they try, [Korean-Americans] cannot avoid the label of forever foreigners, even if they are the third, fourth, or fifth generations who are born in the United States."[29]

Attitudes are changing as America becomes increasingly multicultural. However, we are still in a time in history where we are considered racial minorities, White adjacent, model minorities, and honorary Whites at best.

Pastoring Asian Americans

In light of these trends and experiences, how can the church minister to Asian Americans? Regardless of race and culture, we all, as sinners in need of grace, need the gospel of Jesus. Yet, I believe the emerging generation of Asian Americans, in particular, need the following three gifts of grace.

Tethering

As mentioned earlier, second-generation Asian Americans tend to be a spiritually rootless and mentor-less generation. Although they may not realize it, they need a church to anchor their faith long-term. In many situations moving churches may be necessary and healthy, but cycling through faith communities in every season of life can create a consumerist approach to church. It takes decades to deepen relationships, develop intergenerational discipleship, and experience long-term sanctification.

Too many independent English-speaking Asian American congregations are young and monogenerational. If we take Paul's admonishment in Titus 2:2–8 seriously, our churches will pursue intergenerational worship, in which younger generations can learn to love their spouses and children from older men and women.

May I suggest two aspirations? First, aspire to be as intergenerational as possible. For example, if you are part of an English congregation connected to an immigrant church with older men and women, you are well-positioned to cultivate intergenerational relationships. Look beyond the burden; seek the blessing. If you are an independent young Asian American church plant, consider partnering with a congregation that has older men and women in a formal manner. Some Asian American church plants have partnered and merged with older congregations to bring greater age diversity.

Second, play the long game. If you are leading an Asian American congregation, plan to shepherd your people for decades and not simply for a season. Your church needs you to model what it means to be rooted in a faith community. One of the most important but underappreciated things you can do is stick around. If you, whether as a pastor or layperson, happen to be one of the oldest members of your congregation, you play an extremely important role. As an empty nester or retiree, you have the wisdom and capacity younger men and women can learn from. Welcome the next generation into your life.

Seeing, Hearing, and Understanding

If Asian Americans attend our churches, it may be because they feel seen, heard, and understood. Instead of trying so hard to emulate the majority-culture megachurch, we can steward what God has given to us, including our heritage and the culture, to reach the hearts of the people God brings to us.

I grew up in a Korean-speaking home, spent the bulk of my young life in the Korean church, and sent my kids to Korean-language school. To this day I take my shoes off at home. However, I tried hard to be ethnically neutral in my preaching out of fear of alienating the non-Korean members of my church. It took me years to realize that our church, including the non-Asians, wanted me to be authentic to who I am. This meant settling into my identity as a culturally dissonant individual, husband, and father.

Know the idols and fears of your people. You don't have to frame it as Asian American, but many of the things you idolize and fear inhabit the hearts of your people as well. How can we raise our children to get into a good college? How can I honor my unreasonable aging parent? How can I respond when I experience a bamboo ceiling at work?

We don't brand ourselves as an Asian American church. At the same time, I'm an Asian American pastoring a congregation filled with many who share my background. When the 2021 Atlanta spa shootings happened, we took time in our service to speak the names of the victims and pray for them. It is not something we do often, but it was important to us. We had to weep with them. Through this, many of our people felt seen, heard, and understood.

Belonging

Our members are able to worship from home (WFH). So why do

they skip listening to the best preachers on the internet, drive past other good churches, and come to our church in-person? They are likely not coming for our teaching. They can get better teaching online. For the culturally dissonant, spiritually orphaned Asian American, the need to belong is especially important.

Those in the majority culture have the option to compartmentalize their lives around the different social institutions available to them. Immigrants and minorities, especially from collectivistic societies, long for a community of compatriots.

That is why immigrants and minorities travel farther and linger longer at a church that makes them feel at home. They need more than a sixty-minute megachurch experience as an anonymous audience member. They linger over a cup of coffee with the desire to connect, know, and be known. They want to be with others who understand them without saying a word. They want to break bread (kimchee, dim sum, or sushi) in their home. They want to be missed when they are missing. They need a small group community. Even Asian Americans who attend multicultural or majority-culture megachurches often find each other for spiritual community.

Our primary call as pastors and churches is to "shepherd the flock of God that is among you" (1 Peter 5:2). I encourage you to receive that calling with conviction and confidence. Our (their) Asian Americanness is not a liability to overcome but a calling and opportunity to embrace.

9

Finding Our Voice: Unleashing the Power of Asian American Preaching

by Hanley Liu

Have you ever heard a sermon where the preacher was clearly imitating a popular contemporary preacher? I have; in fact, I've *been* that guy. For the first decade of my preaching ministry, my standard for a good sermon was whether I echoed the content and style of my favorite majority-culture preacher.

When you're first learning, there are certainly benefits to modeling your preaching after other effective preachers. But at some point, you must find your own preaching voice. Preaching with your own voice means preaching out of the wellspring of your God-given personality and life experience. Naturally, this includes tapping into your ethnic and cultural upbringing. For Asian American preachers, this means leveraging our experience to communicate more effectively when preaching to Asian Americans.

Before I say more on the topic of Asian American preaching, it would be very un-Asian of me to not give honor and credit where it is due. Matthew Kim and Daniel Wong have contributed an extremely helpful book on Asian American preaching. If you are looking for a robust discussion on the development of Asian American preaching, I highly recommend *Finding Our Voice: A Vision for Asian North American Preaching.*[30] As an ordinary no-name preacher, my hope is to simply encourage fellow Asian American preachers to speak from the intersection of God's story and our story. As a preacher, you are called to proclaim God's grand story. Yet God has also equipped you with a *personal* story of redemption, which includes your journey and heritage as an Asian American Christian.

Today, Asian American preachers represent different schools and traditions of preaching. For the sake of discussion, let's agree that preaching fundamentally entails the public communication of God's Word. More precisely, Christian preaching aspires to proclaim Christ through Scripture in a manner that is truthful, clear, and relevant.

Most Asian American preachers learn homiletics through a Western framework of communication, which tends to be more direct and linear in thought. East Asians, especially first-generation East Asian immigrants, tend to communicate in more indirect and roundabout ways. At times, the East Asian thought process can be circular. Rather than using imperatives and clearly stating what you *must* do, East Asians will imply what you *ought* to do through stories and life lessons. It's like hinting at an imperative by circling around the command with moral lessons rather than bluntly stating the blunt truth. It is perplexing that many Asian Americans think and communicate in neither fully East Asian nor Western ways. We receive formal theological training in the classrooms of North American seminaries, which is why we often try to emulate the preaching styles of the best majority-culture preachers. But our true communication style—our heart language—is often shaped by a combination of both Western and Eastern values.

My own upbringing took place in an immigrant household, where my parents raised me with a blend of Confucian values and Western ideals. Outside my home, I learned to socialize in a primarily Western context. Consequently, I am trained to process and convey information through that framework. Yet, I am intrinsically attuned to the verbal and nonverbal nuances of East Asian communication. When preaching in an Asian heritage church, I feel an innate connection with the immigrant generation and their American-born children. It's akin to conversing with my mom at the dinner table while she speaks in Mandarin. I respond in English, maintaining all the social cues that would make Confucius proud. My communication style is a blend of both Asian and American cultures without fully embodying either one. Despite my aspirations to sound like the best Christ-centered expository preachers in the Western evangelical world, truthfully, I'm most effective when I am proclaiming Christ and expounding the Scriptures with my God-given Asian American voice.

As Asian American preachers, we can craft sermons that adopt the best of what we learn from Western evangelical preaching styles yet contextualize in a way that connects with the Asian American experience. By contextualization, I mean communicating a message in a way that Asian Americans can best receive it. Although contextualization helps listeners connect with the message, some consider it a departure from faithful exegesis and hermeneutics. So, is it biblical to contextualize our preaching specifically for Asian Americans?

Permission to Contextualize

Christian preachers have practiced culturally distinct contextualization since the beginning of the Church. All Christians share a common faith heritage, one based on New Testament Christianity that has its foundation in Old Testament Judaism. First Peter 2:9 uses Old Testament terminology to express the privilege of knowing Jesus, calling Christians a "chosen race, a royal priesthood, a holy nation," and "a people for his own possession." Although Jewish Christians understood the significance of these terms, gentile Christians needed an explanation. Imagine the earliest New Testament preachers in Asia Minor picking up Peter's letter and discovering the rich meaning behind each of these Jewish terms. To teach these beautiful truths, they had to contextualize—that is, help explain the original context of these statements, not only for Jews but also for gentiles. Early New Testament preachers contextualized a faith heritage, deeply rooted in Old Testament Judaism, to make it accessible and relevant to gentile believers living in the first century.

Since then, numerous preaching frameworks have emerged to contextualize our common faith heritage for diverse cultures, communities, and people groups. Western evangelical preaching, for instance, is just one framework of contextualized preaching that is designed to resonate with the majority culture of the West. Asian American preaching, like African American preaching or Hispanic American preaching, stands equally as a legitimate category of contextualized preaching. To describe preaching as "Asian American" refers to the practice of tailoring sermons to address the specific concerns and experiences of Asians who have either immigrated to or been born in North America. In essence, it's about crafting sermons that speak directly to the unique issues and challenges facing our Asian American communities.

So, do we have permission to contextualize our preaching for Asian Americans? Yes, we have as much permission as the earliest New Testament preachers did. It's the same task completed by Western-Euro-North American preachers centuries ago. Now it's time to collectively step into the pulpit in our own skin because we've been called by God to faithfully expound the Scriptures and herald the gospel for God's glory!

Finding Our Voice

Coming out of seminary, I confess that I tried to mute my Asian American identity in my sermons. I viewed Western majority culture preachers as the standard for good and faithful preaching. Anything that deviated from what was taught in seminary was considered subpar. It's like I was waiting for American seminaries or majority-culture leaders to give me permission to preach from my own Asian American voice. No one ever said I couldn't or shouldn't. It was my own fear of sounding too Asian.

In recent years, I've come to accept that no one is going to give us permission. God has given us permission via our calling to preach. Our local churches affirm that we are qualified and able to teach the Scriptures (1 Tim. 3:1–7; Titus 1:5–9). Yet, it still feels like we're waiting for permission from the larger Western evangelical world to be ourselves in the pulpit. What are we waiting for? Who are we waiting for? Sure, we can wait another generation or two, but no one is going to give us permission to write the next chapter on Asian American preaching. In fact, it would be odd for someone from another culture (or the majority culture) to tell us: "Okay, you have permission to preach from your own God-given Asian American experience." There will be no formal invitation.

The biggest hurdle we face might be our own desire to assimilate into majority culture.

As American Christianity becomes more diverse, consider that the broader evangelical world will be blessed by the collective yet diverse voice of Asian American preachers. Why would we withhold such a gift? No one is going to write our story because it's *our* story. This is our chapter to write. It's our contribution to the story of Christian preaching in America. But it begins by taking ownership of our bicultural Asian American experience.

Preaching from Our Bicultural Experience

To be clear, there is nothing inherently wrong with the Western framework of preaching. When I talk about preaching from our own Asian American voice, I'm not advocating for the adoption of an Eastern or distinctly Asian method of communication. Instead, I'm referring to the nuances that stem from our bicultural experience—a journey that varies among different generations of Asian Americans.

One author aptly defines biculturalism as "having one's foot in two cultural worlds, also known as 'cultural juggling.'"[31] As an Asian American preacher, I deeply resonate with this idea of toggling between two cultures every time I preach.

Recently, I began to identify elements of my preaching that reflect my bicultural upbringing. While the sermon structure, flow of thought, and style of delivery aligns with Western preaching norms, it's the small nuances that reveal my bicultural heritage. Two examples come to mind. First, when I am invited to be a guest preacher, there is an innate tendency to verbally communicate honor toward older individuals in the audience. In majority-culture spaces, I see younger preachers speak very directly and boldly, even challenging an older audience with their commanding presence. As long as they speak respectfully, age seems to be a nonfactor because the preacher is considered qualified by his title, position, or platform. But in Asian spaces with an older crowd, regardless of educational accomplishments or professional title, it's as if I need to apologize for being younger and lacking life experience. Without thinking about it, I adjust my tone to be less direct and commanding.

A second nuance is the careful avoidance of anything that might seem self-promoting. I've attended majority-culture conferences and churches, where it is completely appropriate for the preacher to promote his own book or speak extensively about his achievements. In Asian spaces, especially Asian immigrant churches, this isn't appropriate. It would only be fitting for the moderator, host, or someone else to highlight a speaker's accolades.

Preaching from our bicultural experience can be challenging, yet it presents meaningful opportunities. When preaching to first and second-generation Asian Americans, we can relate with their struggle to fit into broader American society. We can help them see their Asian heritage as God-given. We can expound on the sojourner/foreigner theme from the epistle of 1 Peter (1:1, 2:11) to show the parallel between our Christian journey and our Asian American experience. Our upbringing has prepared us to live for Christ, conditioning our hearts to navigate the tension between biblical values and worldliness. We are perpetual spiritual foreigners looking toward our eternal home in heaven. In this way, God uses our bicultural experience to equip us to battle worldly temptation and endure persecution.

As we seek to steward our bicultural experience through preaching, an ongoing challenge is how to teach multiple generations and cultures. How can we do this well?

Preaching to Multiple Generations and Cultures

Today, Asian American preachers face the growing challenge of preaching to multiple generations with varying cultural perspectives and social values. Consider the recent trend of Asian Americans choosing to stay in or return to healthy Asian heritage churches. This trend will likely continue, thus the task of preparing sermons will inherently demand a more extensive consideration of wider generational and cultural contexts.

Some Chinese heritage churches contain three generations of Asian Americans worshipping as one English congregation. Everyone worships in English. We all read our preferred English Bible translation. We all identify as American (or Canadian), but each generation is culturally distinct.

The first generation includes those who immigrated to North America during their childhood or teenage years, often referred to as the "1.5 Generation." They received their education in Western schools, but their cultural orientation leans toward traditional Asian values. In everyday conversations, you may hear them switch between English and languages like Mandarin, Cantonese, Indonesian, or other dialects. The extent of their assimilation into Western culture depends on their age at the time of immigration.

Those in the second generation were born in North America to immigrant parents. Now, we are witnessing the emergence of the third generation, individuals whose parents and grandparents were also born in North America. Their parents and grandparents may not speak Chinese fluently, which means they are further assimilated into American culture.

Imagine the challenge of trying to connect with each generation at a personal level. First-generation immigrants nod in approval when you express gratitude for how your parents sacrificed everything to start a new life in America. Second-generation listeners will laugh and sigh when you share embarrassing stories of being sent to school with a lunch box full of smelly Asian food. But third-generation listeners might not resonate with those statements. For them, the immigrant experience is just a history lesson. Not to mention that many of their non-Asian friends listen to K-Pop and crave exotic Asian cuisine. The cultural divide between each generation makes it a growing challenge to connect with everyone at the heart level.

The solution is not adopting one style or model of preaching and labeling it "Asian American preaching." Rather, when you preach from your own cultural–generational experience, you will naturally connect with those who share your cultural–generational experience. When we combine our collective voice—across the generations—we can speak to the evolving needs facing Asian Americans.

Your Unique Voice

When we stand behind the pulpit as Asian American preachers, we tell the story of our past, speak prophetically into the challenges of the present, and proclaim Christ as our source of hope for the future. In doing so, we contribute to the next chapter in the story of Asian American Christianity. "Preaching with your Asian American voice" means embracing your personal communication style shaped by your bicultural experience. Your bicultural experience may differ from that of others based on your personal history and generational makeup. In the end, it's about faithfully proclaiming Christ and Scripture in a way that resonates deeply with Asian Americans. We aim to preach in a way that stewards our cultural heritage for the sake of the gospel. We pray that our preaching bridges the gap between cultures to the praise of his glorious grace.

10

Shepherding Singles: Reimagining God's Family in the Church

by Soojin Park

A year ago, my church restructured its leadership model so that every pastor now oversees one major life stage (young adults, families, etc.). After the service that day, I was talking to a sister (let's call her Sarah) in the foyer when she chuckled and mentioned she didn't belong to any of the groups. She was a single woman with no children in her late thirties, so she didn't belong to any of the family-centric groups, but neither was she a young adult. She was gracious enough to make light of the situation, but underneath her laughter was a genuine question: Where do I fit in?

Sarah's situation is common. When you survey the American cultural landscape, institutions—particularly those that serve lower to upper middle class—are designed to best serve those who follow a traditional path of life: school, college, marriage, children. Churches in America, of all ethnic backgrounds, have mirrored this cultural structure. The evangelical church in America upholds this "traditional way of life" more than the broader culture. While a high view of family is good and biblical, churches can forget this isn't the only path for faithful believers. As a result, people like Sarah are considered the exception to the rule and are expected to adapt.

Today, however, people like Sarah are no longer a minority. The number of unmarried working adults has significantly increased in the last few decades. People are getting married later in life or choose not to get married at all. Compared to the 67 percent of adults aged 25–54 that were married in 1990, only 53 percent were married in 2019. In 1980, the median age at first marriage for men was 24 but by 2022 it had risen to 30.[32] Our church pews are increasingly filled with older, single adults who feel awkwardly poised between young adults and families. Unfortunately, many of us are unprepared to handle this steadily growing population in our churches.

As pastors and church leaders, we need to think, pray, and strategize about how to best shepherd these older singles. We can't expect them to bear all the burden of figuring out how to fit in. They need to know their pastors can shepherd them through their particular pains and insecurities. In a world that seems to forget single adults, they need to see that they belong at church. This is especially true for those in an Asian American context. As if being an older single doesn't already carry its fair share of burdens in society and within evangelical culture, Asian American culture adds additional negative connotations. For example, singleness is sometimes seen as a failure to further one's family name and heritage. Often, this feeling of failure deepens because the honor–shame dynamics of Asian cultures deem singleness to be unacceptable. Asian American churches must become safe havens for this growing group in our society to effectively make disciples of *all* demographics.

As an unmarried adult in my thirties and a former staff member of a church, I speak from experience from both sides of this concern. Even as someone who should be well-connected within the church, as I slid into my thirties, I often felt unsure of my place in the congregation. I asked myself, "If I wasn't on staff, where would I belong here?" Sometimes I felt like the pastors and elders, all being married with children, didn't understand what life as an older single was like and didn't know how to minister to us. I dreaded conversations with older adults, knowing the well-intended but poorly executed question—"Why are you still single?"—would inevitably come up. Did they really believe that because I was single that my life was incomplete? Having said all this, I also know how quickly the single population has grown and how daunting it can be to care for them well. This new ministry territory lacks a clear road map. Therefore, I want to humbly offer three ways that your church could grow to become a home for older singles.

Cultivate a Culture that Dignifies Singleness

If you ask any Bible-literate Christian whether singleness is a gift, they will likely say yes. They know this is the right Sunday school answer that comes from 1 Corinthians 7. However, it is rare to find a church that actively welcomes, accepts, and celebrates singleness as a true gift from God. Paul's words on singleness are often thrown as a bone to those who desperately want to be married. But they're rarely used to bless someone.

When was the last time you told someone they were blessed to be single like we tell people they're blessed to be married or blessed to have a child? Even with the best intentions, we sometimes contribute to a low view of singleness by treating it as a trial to be endured or a prerequisite for marriage. This makes it difficult for older singles to thrive and to really feel they belong. Although few pastors blatantly denigrate singleness, the lack of a culture that properly dignifies it makes church unappealing and unwelcoming to singles. So, although most people in our churches will get married (and we should celebrate that), let's be mindful of how we think and talk about singleness.

Every church has a culture. I'm a firm believer that leadership, particularly the pastors, shape that culture. The values held at the top trickle down to members. This means that you, as a leader, have a tremendous opportunity to influence the culture of your church. Start with the language you use about singleness, both in and out of the pulpit. Instead of assuming marriage is a given for all congregants, recognize that marriage may not be for everyone, whether by choice or involuntarily. As you empathize with those who long for marriage, also point to the gifts of singleness. Instead of asking singles about dating and marriage, ask them about their jobs, hobbies, and families to show their lives are full, even without a spouse. In addition to celebrating engagements and weddings, make it a habit to really celebrate other milestones in the lives of singles (starting or finishing school, getting a new job, accomplishing a lifelong goal, finishing a marathon, getting through a really difficult situation, major birthdays, etc.). Rather than saying singles should serve more now because they have time, highlight those who are serving and call others to steward their life stage similarly. As you actively change your own language around singleness, you will teach your church to see and speak of singleness in the right way.

These changes might seem small, but collectively, they help show singles they're not in a permanent state of waiting for something else; their lives are valuable and worthy of celebration now. Jesus was single all his life. So was Paul, the author of most of the New Testament. Scripture attests to the fact that single life is just as meaningful as married life. This can bring much comfort and healing to weary singles lacking validation by their church community. We have an opportunity to share this hope with the growing population of singles, but we must help our churches create a new posture toward singleness. As a single, nothing makes me feel more dignified than when older members of our church choose to engage in rich conversations with me about my life—with no questions or concerns about if or when I will be married. When they ask about my ministry, my family, or my dog, and want to genuinely know how I'm doing, it is a small but significant reminder that to them I have a full life. When my pastors ask for my opinion on a recent theological issue, laugh with me about a new Korean drama, or share their big dreams for me in my ministry journey, it reminds me I am a whole member of the church and the staff. Pastors and leaders, let's create this kind of culture for the singles in our churches.

See God's Family in a New Way

The Bible is clear about the importance of the nuclear family and the various roles that people play within it. I believe our churches have done a great job emphasizing this. There are sermon series, seminars, and conferences for parenting, family ministry, and marriage across the country. While this is good, I believe this focus has often overshadowed a proper emphasis on the priority of *God's family*. Jesus emphasizes the importance of loving our family members and honoring them. Yet he also teaches that marriage bonds will not exist in heaven (Mark 12:18–25). The bond formed in his blood, through faith, is more important than that of earthly families (Mark 3:31–35). He clarifies that what lasts in eternity is not our nuclear families but our spiritual family that is united in him. Sadly, our churches do not always reflect this reality. Many of our congregants idolize the nuclear family, spending all their time and energy on their own children and spouses, without considering their church family.

Not only does this exacerbate a single person's feeling of inferiority, but it also can be very lonely for someone to be part of a church without a family of their own. If everyone is caring for their own families, who cares for singles? And who can the singles care for? Who do singles spend their holidays with and who will check in on them when they don't show up to church? Of course, singles can care for each other, but for the church to truly be family, there must be intentional effort to integrate the lives of single and married people. To help singles belong and to shepherd them well, your church must grow in its collective identity as a family. Once again, it must be a cultural shift that starts from the top. From the pulpit, there must be an emphasis on the church as family and how we are to intentionally love and serve one another. As a pastor or leader, you must demonstrate to your church what it can look like.

You don't have to abandon your family or exhaust your schedule. It can be as simple as integrating your church members into the life of your family with small things. Invite singles to your home for casual dinners. Ask the young newlywed couple to watch your kids for date night, then ask them to stay and chat over dessert. Encourage older couples in your church to invite younger singles and couples to join the mundane parts of their family's day-to-day life. The more people share in everyday life, the more they will see each other as family and learn to care for each other.

For older singles, especially those who still long for a family of their own, singleness can feel like a painful and lonely burden. As they struggle to find their place in the world alone, wouldn't it be wonderful if they could feel at home in God's family within our churches? I read about a man who struggled with same-sex attraction who knew he would never be married and have his own family. The one thing that helped him endure this was the friendships he formed in his church. They acted as his family. This is the kind of gospel hope churches can offer to those who are involuntarily single and enduring painful seasons of waiting. If we truly live out our identity as God's family, we become a place where singles, although lonely at times, know they are seen and loved.

Create Spaces for Older Singles to be Seen and Known

While families stick together and care for each other, every part of the family still has its own concerns and needs. In the church, every demographic—whether parents with young children, empty nest-ers, or singles—has unique needs, fears, and idols. So, although the church family should be integrated, there still should be spaces for these various groups to not only connect with each other but also to be heard and seen by leadership.

Like Sarah, a lot of older singles fall through the cracks between ministries because they don't quite fit in with any existing group in the church. Their struggles are vastly different from those of singles in their early to midtwenties, and they can't identify with their peers who are starting families with young children. Without intentional effort from leadership to reach this demographic, some may drift away from the church or stick it out despite ongoing loneliness.

Whether there are two older singles in your church or a hundred, I encourage you to carve out space and time to care for these individuals. This could be a monthly gathering for a large group or a meal with one older single in your congregation. Regardless of what it looks like, the important thing is that the older singles have a place where their unique struggles, pains, and fears are validated and addressed through the lens of the gospel. They want to know that pastors and church leaders are aware of the unique challenges they face. And, like everyone, they desperately need gospel-centered guidance and encouragement in their lives. In addition to creating spaces for singles in your church programming, remember them in your preaching. Sermon illustrations tend to ignore this demographic, so addressing them is a small but powerful way to care for singles.

Our God is *El Roi*, the God who sees the forgotten ones and lifts them up (Gen. 16:13). We may be small in the universe, yet he knows each of us intimately. When we intentionally care for the singles among us, we reflect the heart of God.

A Beautiful Calling

As I close out this chapter, I want to plead with you—pastors and ministry leaders—to not see my words as an added burden to your ministry responsibilities. It can be so easy to read about new trends or shifts in demographics and think, "Great, this is just another thing I'm not doing." This isn't a burden; it's an exciting opportunity God has given you to do effective gospel ministry. It's an open door. Singles wrestle with questions of belonging—questions the gospel can answer. Where these individuals don't fit into the traditional mold of American institutions or Asian cultural norms, the church can welcome them in as cherished members of God's family. May God give you a growing heart for this demographic and equip you to be a shepherd for the singles in your community.

11

Creative Legacy: Navigating Ministry
in a Changing World

by Cory K. Ishida

I was born to Nisei parents (second-generation Japanese Americans). I am a Sansei. I was sent to a Japanese American Presbyterian Church as a child by nonbelieving parents, where I learned what it meant to be a part of an ethnic-based community of believers—even though I never confessed faith in Christ.

I grew up a Christianized agnostic through my college years. I got saved in my wife's Disciples of Christ church made up of Midwestern non-Asians. I was mentored by a seminary student named John Wells who, unbeknownst to me, was training me for ministry.

One year after my baptism at age 22, God called me into pastoral ministry. I had no idea what to do next, so I served as the youth director of a non-Asian youth group.

Looking back, many of my experiences, like being Associated Student Body (ASB) president at my high school which required me to be the master of ceremonies at every school assembly, prepared me for what God had in store for my adult life.

Preparation for Asian American Ministry

My cousin got saved at a Christian conference at Mount Hermon and asked me to start a Bible study at her home church (which happened to be the church I grew up in). I agreed and was reintroduced to the Christian world of my cultural heritage as a follower of Christ.

I became their youth director and learned about ministering to teenage Japanese Americans. Through trial and error, along with the prompting of the Holy Spirit, I learned how to reach people with the gospel in a Japanese American context.

In March 1977, the Lord directed me to leave my employment as a pharmaceutical sales representative and go into full-time ministry as a preaching pastor with no seminary education. Facing the impossible, like Jehoshaphat (2 Chronicles 20), I sought the Lord realizing that the battle belonged to God, not to me.

During the time of unemployment, through providential circumstances, I was offered the position of senior pastor of Evergreen Baptist Church. They must have been desperate. On May 1, 1977, I became the interim senior pastor of Evergreen Baptist Church in East Los Angeles. Worship attendance was hovering around forty people, of which about eight of them were young adults under the age of thirty. By faith, they made me their permanent senior pastor in November 1977.

The Importance of Change

While I was the youth director at the Japanese American Presbyterian Church, I tried to do things in ways that were unorthodox in a Nisei-driven church. I was constantly told that "things aren't done that way," like guitars in worship service or altar calls during service. I learned that nothing happens unless leadership is willing to change. I became convinced that pouring new wine into old wineskins would result in exactly what Jesus says would happen in Mark 2:22. The new wine (young people coming to Christ) will bleed out the old wineskin (traditions and customs of the older generation church).

Japanese American and Chinese American churches, although orthodox and quite loving, appeared to be bastions of customs and traditions that impeded the movement of gospel into the hearts and minds of young people. Things would have to change, but change is difficult and always comes at a price.

The Winds of Change at Evergreen

I had four strong convictions when I started as senior pastor of Evergreen: the power of prayer, the priority of preaching the Word of God, the importance of leadership being willing to change, and that what many sincere Japanese American and Chinese American churches were doing wasn't working. Young people were leaving in droves.

One of the first things I asked the faithful leadership at Evergreen was: Do we want to grow the church? I asked them to think about it carefully. Growth would mean five things. First, they would no longer know everyone by name, and their church of forty would no longer be comfortable. Second, they would eventually need to hand over leadership to others. Third, the culture and the climate at Evergreen would change from a mom-and-pop church to a growing community of faith. Fourth, the way we worshipped the Lord would be different as we contemporized the worship services (percussion instruments, here we come). Fifth, we would likely shift from a Japanese American church into an Asian American church.

Thankfully, the leadership of Evergreen was willing to change. When people ask me why Evergreen grew, I tell them that we prayed, preached the Word of God, and embraced change. One key element greatly enabled Evergreen to transform from a Japanese American Church to an Asian American church. In the 1950s, the English-speaking component of the ministry grew exponentially after World War II. As a result, the Japanese-speaking division split off and formed a new church across the street in East Los Angeles. This was a huge factor in Evergreen becoming an Asian American church. Because we were English-speaking only, we dealt with cross-generational issues without the cross-cultural challenges faced by most of our sister Asian churches.

Why Asian American?

As I mentioned before, about eight young adults faithfully attended Evergreen when I started. Four of them were Chinese Americans, two of the young men were our most gifted Bible teachers and mentors, and one of them was our most talented guitarist.

This made it quite natural to move from being a Japanese American ministry to an Asian American ministry. We eventually moved away from all joint activities with the Japanese-speaking church across the street, which still had first-generation parents of our second-generation members. We took the posture of supporting them in any way we could without doing ministry jointly with them.

I also held a deep conviction that the Japanese American church had seen its day. I read a report in the early 1980s explaining that most Japanese immigrants were businesspeople and their families planned to stay in the United States for a short period of time.

Simultaneously, out-marriages of Japanese American young adults were at an all-time high. It was time to develop an Asian American ministry to capture the lost and recover those leaving bilingual, bicultural churches.

Before long, the ministry of Evergreen grew, and we began holding two worship services of more than 200 worshippers each in a church building constructed to accommodate one hundred people. The Lord kept bringing Asian Americans, and they were getting saved and growing in faith.

A Game Changer

The time came to hire an associate pastor as the ministry continued to grow. This decision was a crossroad in the life of the church. We had more than outgrown our facility and needed to expand in the community or move to where a large portion of our church family resided in the San Gabriel Valley.

I asked our leadership and our church family to make two decisions simultaneously. We could either stay and hire a Hispanic associate pastor since our surrounding community was 90 percent Hispanic, or we could move and hire our current intern who was Chinese American.

We unanimously decided to move and call Ken Fong as our first associate pastor. This was a game changer. We were now on an undeniable course as an Asian American church.

The Keys to Growth

I am often asked, "Why did Evergreen dramatically grow while other Japanese and Chinese churches did not?" The question had a flaw—I was being asked to compare apples to oranges. We were *not* like the other churches. We were very different.

We tried to honor our cultural heritage without being bound by them. Jesus proclaimed, "He has sent me to proclaim liberty to the captives and recovering of sight to the blind, to set at liberty those who are oppressed" (Luke 4:18). There are many ways to be held captive, blind, and oppressed. Tradition and adherence to culture can be captivating, blinding, and oppressive to the movement of the gospel within a people group. I considered English-speaking Asian Americans a people group that needed to hear the gospel and have their lives changed by the power of Christ and his Word.

We de-emphasized culture and traditions and emphasized the preaching of God's Word within the context of being Asian American. We sang contemporary songs of praise, some of which were written by Asian Americans. We used guitars, drums, and keyboards. We emphasized missionary endeavors to our motherlands of Japan and China. We targeted English-speaking Asian Americans as we evangelized. As far as I know, we were one of the few churches doing ministry in this fashion. The net result was that the Lord grew us in number and spiritual vitality.

The Message

Earlier I wrote that I emphasized the preaching of God's Word within the context of being Asian American. What did that look like?

The illustrations that I used to elucidate the Scriptures were naturally Asian American in context. I am an Asian American, so my life reflected the journey of an Asian American born and raised in America. I preached on subjects that spoke into the lives of Asian Americans. They could see how the Word of God addressed issues that were important to Asian Americans and not just White America.

I would repeatedly get the comment, "You don't preach

like an Asian American." I wasn't quite sure what to make of that statement. I was criticized by Asian American seminarians for "sounding like a White preacher." To some, I was not a good example or model for English-speaking Asian Americans. How does a prototypical Asian American preacher sound? I sounded like me—an English-speaking Asian American. I suppose the net result of earlier years of ministry at Evergreen involved the breaking of stereotypical thinking. I once preached at a mostly White church and an elderly lady came up to me afterward and said, "You speak very good English for an Oriental." She meant it with kindness and a good heart, but I chuckled inside.

Throughout my tenure as senior pastor, I consistently taught on marriage and family. I loved teaching from God's Word on how to raise children. We poured resources into children and teenage ministries. Ultimately, this resulted in Asian American families gravitating to Evergreen because of the importance of family in their lives.

When I preached on my personal journey into father wounds, father loss, and father yearnings, this resonated deeply with my people, because many Asian Americans long for reconciliation with their earthly fathers.

The Internship Program

From the very outset, I resolved to train pastors, so we developed an internship program while we were still a fledgling church.

During the congregational meeting in which we voted on funding an internship program, one member stood up to express his concern. "Why," he wondered "would we invest funds in training pastors and leaders who would eventually leave us since we couldn't hire all of them?" I simply stated that we needed to be kingdom-minded and bless the larger community of Christ with workers who were trained and ready to serve within the Asian American community. I also believed that a sign of a healthy, vital church is the development of full-time workers for the kingdom. Disciples beget disciples and shepherds beget shepherds, much like Paul and Timothy.

The Lord blessed us with a multitude of lives fully devoted to loving God through full-time church ministry. Ultimately, we trained about one hundred interns for a variety of ministry positions over forty-two years.

Church Planting

As a church, Evergreen was committed to growing the kingdom within the Asian American community. To do this, we planted churches with the same mission and vision.

From the internship program, we trained pastors who would be willing to plant a church. We challenged members from within our church family to take a step of faith and become a part of a new church plant. We guaranteed the funding of our church plants for two years and made sure they were funded adequately before becoming independent.

One of the hardest things for any parent to do is release their children when the time comes. The church plants were our children. We blessed them, and they were a blessing to us.

The First Move

We believed the Lord was leading us into the San Gabriel Valley. In 1987, we bought and built the first phase on a three-acre piece of property in the city of Rosemead. During our interim stay at the Narramore Christian Foundation property, we grew to almost 900 worshippers. When we finally moved to our new church home, we were averaging 1,200 worshippers and had already outgrown the new site.

The move to the San Gabriel Valley gave greater access to the Asian American community in the San Gabriel area and solidified our calling to reach Asian Americans for Christ.

The Hive

By mid-1990's, we were bursting at the seams and were just too big for our site. While seeking a solution in prayer, the Lord spoke to me very clearly. He said to "split" the church. Because the word *split* has such negative connotations in regard to a church congregation, we called it a hive.

No one in leadership wanted to "hive," but after a year-long season of prayer and discussion, the hive was initiated and implemented in 1997. Evergreen SGV was born with me being the senior pastor along with 300 faithful adventurers.

Our mission was to reach Asian Americans for Christ in the greater San Gabriel Valley area. We met for ten years at Rio Hondo Community College. The Lord blessed our ministry, and we grew. In 2007, we purchased a preexisting church that had once been a school. The seventeen-acre parcel with renovated buildings provided a home for Evergreen SGV. We grew to over 1,200 worshippers and planted six churches over the years with the same mission.

In 2019, the Lord called me into retirement. After a year of rest, I felt called to serve Asian American churches and ministries whenever and wherever I can. I am amazed at the opportunities that the Lord continues to provide to serve him and the population to which I have been called.

Final Reflections

I am filled with wonder at the providential hand of God throughout my life. He nurtured me, gifted me to become a pastor, and called me to serve as a shepherd of his flock.

I wanted to become a sports coach, but I became a coach of a different kind. The Lord molded me to become a teacher–trainer of spiritual (rather than athletic) disciplines. Although I initially thought I would be a shepherd of a multiracial church family, the Lord directed me with unswerving certainty to serve a people group in which I was an active participant.

The apostle Paul wrote, "To the Jews I became as a Jew, in order to win Jews" (1 Cor. 9:20). These words resonated in my heart and soul as I pursued the ministry to which God called me. I suppose my pastoral epitaph could say: "To Asian Americans I became as an Asian American, that I might win Asian Americans."

So, what about the future of Asian American ministries?

I once had a non-Asian professor in seminary who stated there should be no ethnic churches and that we should all be one church. After class, my associate went up to him and asked, "Well, professor, when will you start coming to our church?" Needless to say, he never showed up.

As long as immigration from Asian countries exists, children of those immigrants will assimilate into American culture. For them, the presence of Americanized Asian churches and ministries can provide the clarion call of the gospel and a place to call home.

Soli Deo Gloria.

PART III

THE ASIAN AMERICAN LEADER

12

Heart Matters: Unmasking Idols in Asian American Leadership

by Kim N. Kira

"Your preaching is killing the church, and it's not just me who thinks so."

Although I didn't believe it was necessarily true (our church hadn't died yet), I still vividly remember the pain of that comment. Grief, insecurity, anger, discouragement, pride—they were all there. I struggled to respond to this disgruntled church member. But in reality the issue ran much deeper, because it was about what was going on in my heart. If we are going to be faithful to our calling as Asian American leaders,[33] we must realize that being Asian isn't just a matter of what goes on *around* us, but what goes on *within* us.[34]

The Heart of the Issue
To truly consider the heart of the Asian American leader, we must first have a biblical understanding of the heart. The heart is more than our feelings and affections. Biblically, the heart is who we are at the

deepest level (Prov. 4:23). It's our mind, will, affections, and morals. And significantly, our hearts determine how we understand, interpret, and respond to life. As Jesus said, "out of the abundance of the heart his mouth speaks" (Luke 6:45). This means our response to the joys and challenges of ministry (in an Asian context or otherwise), is determined by our hearts. Whether grateful for a compliment from a member, disheartened by criticism, grieved by the suffering of a member, embittered toward someone we serve with, excited about growth, or discouraged by a decline in numbers, our response originates in the heart.

In Romans 1:25, Paul diagnoses why the heart is sick so often: "because they exchanged the truth about God for a lie and worshiped and served the creature rather than the Creator, who is blessed forever! Amen." Paul asserts we are always worshipping, and we really only have two choices of what we will worship: the Creator or creation. We will either worship our triune God or some idol.

An idol is anything that we worship in the place of God (e.g., people's approval, comfort, money, success). This is not an abstract theological idea, because what we worship determines how we live (Rom. 1:21–32; James 4:1–4; Matt. 22:24–40). Every moment is lived out of what matters to us, what is important to us, and what holds our affections. If we worship Christ, we will live in joyful obedience to our God. But if we worship a counterfeit god, we will experience the struggle and pain that comes from sin.

Our Worship Precedes Our Asianness

Idolatry is alive and well in every culture, so as Asian American church leaders, what idols are silently pulling at our hearts? What tends to develop and deepen them? And most important, how do we keep them from derailing us?

A good starting place is to recognize that the worship of hearts is more fundamental to who we are than any Asian identity we may possess. If the way we live is a result of our worship, then we should assess our Asianness through the lens of how it influences our worship. Our cultural heritage can significantly impact our hearts and therefore impact how we view, process, understand, and respond to the various joys and trials of ministry.[35]

What does this look like practically?[36] For many who grow up in an Asian American context, there is a great priority placed on being successful according to the world's standards and in a way that reflects well on the family. This can extend to many areas of life, but often it's those things that are more public and can be seen (like academics, occupation, music). For many of us, worldly success wasn't just a virtue, it was the ultimate virtue. We learned to pursue it at all costs, even to the detriment of things that truly mattered. This means that it can be particularly difficult in an Asian American context to recognize success as an idol.

The lure of success can be exacerbated by the honor–shame culture so many of us were raised in. In most Asian cultures, reputation is foundational to identity. As a result, the pursuit of honor and the fear of shame guides everything we do. Our parents are often the greatest enforcers of this. The fear of bringing shame on our families drives us to relentlessly pursue success so we can attain honor, respect, and status. We receive the greatest praise for our successes and the greatest condemnation for our failures. The importance of success is framed as a matter of right or wrong, honor or shame, even earning love or losing it. So, our parents didn't just tolerate rival gods in our households; they encouraged them. This idolatrous worship was often the air we breathed.[37]

The idolatrous bent of our culture is a complicated reality. Although there may be selfish motives behind our parents' desires (e.g., concern over how their children reflect on them), it is often intermingled with a kind of love, misguided though it may be. Parents want their kids to do well and be happy, which in their minds can only come through success defined by the world's standards (e.g., financial prosperity). Outwardly, this desire seems innocuous, maybe even loving. After all, who in the world complains about success? But when we recognize the fundamental nature of the heart's worship, the gleam of worldly success starts to tarnish, and the idolatry underneath starts to show.

When we go into ministry, the idol of success is camouflaged under a veneer of serving Jesus.[38] I use the word *camouflage* because most pastors don't announce, "I do this to gain success." Rather, we know enough to hide it under language about pursuing God's glory, producing fruit, winning converts, or cultivating growth (spiritual, not numerical, of course). Likely these are true; these hopes aren't completely absent. But intermingled with them is a desire for worldly success. We want people to admire and approve of us. We want numerical growth because it reflects well on us. We hate criticism (even helpful criticism), and we love compliments. The dark and dangerous reality of our misplaced worship comes to light when we realize we can be preaching about the glory of God and simultaneously seeking our own glory. What complicates it all is that because public appearances matter so much and outward humility is important, we are then encouraged to deflect the attention and compliments we so desperately crave.

In light of this, our Asian culture is not just the context of ministry, but by influencing our worship, it shapes us at the deepest level of who we are. And if we are not careful, we will mindlessly bow down to the idols our culture props up.

When Our Idols Are Threatened

Idolatrous worship also explains why the challenges of ministry can lead to so many of our internal struggles. We struggle with fear, stress, and anger when our idols are threatened.[39] For example, if my idol of success is threatened in some way (through criticism, declining numbers, difficult staff relationships, etc.), then I will be beset by any number of sinful and negative emotions.

Jesus highlights this principle in Matthew 6. Right before he commands us to, "not be anxious" in verse 25, he says, "No one can serve two masters" in verse 24. Jesus ties together idolatry and anxiety. His audience was anxious because their idol (money) was threatened by their poverty. The only way they could avoid being anxious was if they had only one master: their heavenly Father.

This dynamic explains our struggles in ministry. Ministry has the potential to feed our idolatry in times of flourishing, and it has the potential to threaten and even devastate our idols in times of difficulty. Consider all the ways that the idol of success can be threatened: low attendance, critique and complaints, relational tension, tight budgets, lack of encouragement, and so on.

This was never truer in my ministry than during the pandemic, which was the hardest season of ministry I have ever experienced. On one hand it was hard because of the suffering of our people and the challenge of making wise decisions, but when I say it was a hard season, I'm specifically referring to the devastation of my idols. It was truly painful. For example, as a people pleaser, I wanted to make wise decisions that aligned with my people's desires (previously, they usually did). Then suddenly, with the arrival of the pandemic, I had to make decisions knowing someone would be unhappy. Beyond that, size and growth became somewhat hidden. (How do YouTube views even translate?) Perhaps the worst part was the critique. Although our church was gracious and very supportive, those few voices of dissent seemed the most prominent. Because of my idols of success and people's approval, if 100 people agreed with us but one didn't, that one rang the loudest in my ears and echoed the longest in my heart. It would be easy to blame specific people or circumstances, but truthfully it was my idols being laid to waste—not the trials or the critique—that made that season difficult.

As Asian American leaders, we have to recognize that while our culture does not cause us to have idols, like every culture, it often creates a unique environment for our idols to flourish and grow. And when these idols are threatened by the challenges and suffering of ministry, it produces fear, stress, and anger.

The Gospel

What then is our hope since we can't change how we were raised? Our only hope is the gospel we preach every week. Paul says this in Galatians 6:14, "But far be it from me to boast except in the cross of our Lord Jesus Christ, by which the world has been crucified to me, and I to the world." We understand that Christ was crucified, and that we are crucified with Christ, but Paul uses the imagery differently here. He says "the *world* has been crucified to me" (my emphasis). The world in this context refers to the unredeemed creation, the present evil age, those things opposed to God. Paul is saying, "That world is dead to me." In other words, we no longer have to worship at its altars or sacrifice to its idols. The power of the gospel frees us to worship Christ rightly, and when we do, we hope and live rightly.

Applying this great reality to our example of the idol of success, when the gospel transforms our hearts, we no longer need the idol of success to provide what we think we need (security, affirmation, acceptance, approval, hope, etc.), because we find all those things in Christ through the gospel.

How does the gospel actually transform the idolatries of Asian American pastors? There are many ways to apply the gospel to this issue,[40] but let's consider a couple that specifically address the issue of idolatry.

Meditate on Christ More Than You Meditate on Your Idols

We must orient our hearts away from our idols toward Christ. As Colossians 3:2 describes, we set our mind on things of earth. For example, when we receive a critical email, we are tempted to meditate on it. We reread it. We ruminate over it. We play it out like a courtroom scene in our heads and make sure we are always declared righteous. When we see the person who sent it, we let our minds wander and convince ourselves not just that we are right and they are wrong but that we are good and they are bad. It's like doing personal devotions rooted in bitterness, worry, and discouragement. Remember, part of the point of personal devotions is to pursue a deeper relationship, to grow in affection and love, and to turn our hearts toward others. And this is happening, but toward our idols. With this deeper affection for our idols, our anxiety, fear, and anger grow.

We need to have gospel truth ready to meditate on when we are tempted to dwell on the wrong things. When I am tempted to meditate on the false narrative the world offers ("you are your successes" or "you need people to like you to be happy"), I find it helpful to have truth ready to meditate on instead. I try to set my mind on things above, not on earthly things. For example, every week during the last worship song before I preach (when I'm tempted to worry what people think), I pray the same thing: "Lord help me preach *to* love, not to *be* loved." Why? Because I am loved. When I preach to be loved, I worry so much. When I know I am loved by God and preach to love Christ and our church family, I experience the freedom that comes with that.

We Must See Threats to Ministry as Grace

If stress, fear, and anger come from our idols being threatened, we must reconsider the real nature of those threats. We need a theology of suffering, rooted in the gospel, so we don't see the trials, difficulties, and even failures of ministry as threats but as God's grace to accomplish his loving, wise, and at times painful plan for our lives (1 Peter 1:6–7; James 1:2–4). Since we know nothing can separate us from the love of Christ (Rom. 8:38–39), we trust that nothing passes into our life that hasn't first passed through the filter of his love. God is always at work, even in the difficulties of life. Absolutely nothing is wasted in his economy. Although he is likely accomplishing thousands of things through each trial we face, at least one is humbling us so that we would draw near to him in faith, love, and worship. When we believe this, it means we will understand that those threats to our success are actually acts of grace defeating the idols that endanger our souls.

Two things encourage humility: the first is to repent. If you don't own your sin, you will be stuck in it. As we say in our counseling class, "When there is a lack of repentance, sanctification comes to a grinding halt." So, for example, if you justify your lack of love because of what the other person has done, you will not change. Or if you justify your sinful worry because of how challenging ministry is, you will not change. However, if you own your sin through repentance, you will experience the grace that God gives to the humble (James 4:6–10). I often pray, "Lord, forgive me for so being so concerned about what people think about me. Help me to see your glory, not mine."

Second, meditate on truth when you are tempted to meditate on your suffering. The love of God is the first lesson we learn in Sunday school, but in reality, it is so deep we are wading in the shallow end of the pool of that doctrine. For me, this means reminding myself that whatever is happening is God loving me. As Spurgeon said, "Remember this: Had any other condition been better for you than the one in which you are, divine love would have put you there."[41] For example, when a family leaves the church and I am tempted to be discouraged or worry, I set my mind on things above. I remind myself, "Lord, since nothing can separate me from your love, this family leaving the church is you loving me." I meditate on the reality that God doesn't love me despite trials; he loves me *in* them. So I need to believe that a family leaving (as painful as that might be), is still God's kindness to me.

A Superior Love

I pray that this chapter will provide a starting point to consider how your culture has influenced your heart, and how the gospel can reorient your worship back to Christ. The only way to defeat the inferior worship of our idols is through the superior worship of Christ. That is our only hope for the true and lasting transformation that allows us to lead and serve with a deeper sense of peace and joy.

13

Silencing Shame: The Fear of
Not Being Good Enough

by Harold Y. Kim

Before COVID hit in the spring of 2020, I hit an implacable wall. I lost all motivation in pastoral ministry as a culmination of deep weariness and stress compounded by bouts of insomnia, depression, and suicidal ideation. Encouraged by family, friends, and my church to take a sabbatical and seek professional counseling, I realized it was more than a midlife crisis. For much of my life, I've battled shame. While shame can be appropriate and even redemptive, mine was debilitating. I was terrified of failure. In this, I'm far from alone in the Asian American community.

In his book, *Now I Become Myself,* Pastor Ken Shigematsu explains the connection between shame and his lifelong fear of "not being enough."[42] This fear comes in countless forms: the fear of not being American or Asian enough, accomplished enough, strong enough, attractive enough, or blessed enough. Fill in the blank.

As a pastor, my greatest shame has to do with the fear of *not being enough of a pastor*. This was intensified by a series of losses early on at Christ Central of Southern California (CCSC). In one year, we lost three brothers to suicides and an accident. I mourned as best I could, but mostly I felt responsible, like *I* had failed. I tried to move forward with my default mode in life—get busy enough to bury it, and do meaningful and redemptive things to make up for it. Looking back, that year was an eerie repetition of how I had dealt with my father's sudden death during college. Rather than dealing with loss and a sense of failure in honest ways, I tried to simply become a better pastor, which ironically, nearly brought an end to pastoring itself.

Through my sabbatical, God began teaching me how to deal with shame. First and foremost, I've learned to name my shame. I talk more transparently and regularly about shame with family, friends, and leaders at church. What a gift from God! As I talk more about it, there is growing clarity into what is really going on inside of me. And as people listen, they offer much needed perspective, comfort, and relief as well. Galatians 6:2 commands us to "bear one another's burdens." When you unload burdens with those who care like Jesus does, your burden is not only lightened but hope and courage are restored.

In Japan, a common condition called "karoshi" refers to sudden death from overwork. In October 2022, Forbes detailed symptoms of karoshi in post-COVID America in "10 Signs You Could Be Working Yourself to Death In A Hybrid World."[43] The article discussed constant hurry, irritability, and perfectionism. While death may not occur, how do symptoms of karoshi appear? A very high sense of responsibility coupled with the fear of burdening others creates an unbearable burden of your own. I haven't met an Asian American minister or leader who does not suffer both. If this resonates with you, please find someone you can begin to share with. If life seems unbearable to you, please seek professional help immediately.

Second, I have immensely benefited from Christian professional counseling. Disclaimer: one size or counselor does not fit all. For leaders in ministry, unfortunately, there are very few safe spaces in which to be completely free to say all that you want and say all that you mean. In the company of an experienced and gifted counselor, I have gained self-awareness, invaluable insight about my family of origin, the ability to better understand and accept others, and wisdom to navigate complex crises and leadership challenges.

However, the most helpful practice has been talking to God and hearing God talk to me. The psalms of lament, in particular, have become my prayer template. Beyond reading or memorizing the psalms (as transformative as those habits are), I've learned to personalize and interact with the saddest psalms, allowing the Holy Spirit to translate, add, expand, and specify the prayer with words of my own, and my own with the psalmist's. Through this practice, I've experienced God's personal healing presence for my shame like never before. Psalm 31 provides an ideal template for anyone seeking relief from shame:

> In you, O Lord, do I take refuge;
>> let me never be put to shame;
>> in your righteousness deliver me! (v. 1)

Having studied in American seminaries on both coasts, I learned a lot about guilt. Guilt is the legal and objective status for every sinner before Holy God. By the sheer grace of God, divine acquittal or salvation is offered through faith in the person and work of Jesus Christ, not in ourselves, to the glory of God (Eph. 2:8–10; Rom. 3:23–25). This gospel is good news for the guilty.

But sin brings guilt *and* shame. I recall learning very little about shame in seminary classes, and this left a huge gap in my understanding and experience of the gospel. In paraphrasing Brené Brown in *Daring Greatly*, shame says: "I am not worthy or good enough for love, belonging or connection. I'm unlovable, I do not belong."[44] In the Netflix series *Beef*, Amy Lau, a self-made yet self-loathing entrepreneur, is haunted by the voice of shame via an imaginary witch: "I can't tell anyone your secrets because no one would love you."[45]

Guilt is an individualistic and legal verdict over something done wrong, and shame is the social and inescapable feeling of being unlovable. According to Dr. Brown's research, guilt can provide motivation for improvement and change, but debilitating, recurring shame rarely produces healthy outcomes. Nobody survives the spiral of shame without hating and hurting themselves. They often succumb to depression, rage, disorders, hopelessness, or hating and hurting others.

David admits that much of his shame was the consequence of sin:

For my life is spent with sorrow,
    and my years with sighing;
my strength fails because of my iniquity,
    and my bones waste away. (Ps. 31:10)

Despite the evangelical tendency to assume the heroes of the Bible are strong moral examples, David, the author of Psalm 31, was deeply compromised. David was guilty of raping Bathsheba. In his coverup, David orchestrated the death of her husband during the heat of battle. David also suffered shame as a failing king and father. But David also suffered much undeserved shame based on slander:

For I hear the whispering of many—
    terror on every side!—

as they scheme together against me,
>> as they plot to take my life. (Ps. 31:13)

In verse 18, he cries out to God:

Let the lying lips be mute.

In the throes of shame, many try to ignore or cover their shame with excessive work, busyness, consumption, and entertainment. They try to escape it by changing relationships, jobs, cities, and churches. Some camouflage shame with acts of religious piety and charity, hoping it will disappear. But for David as well, shame was unrelenting.

For my life is spent with sorrow,
>> and my years with sighing. (Ps. 31:10)

So what does the psalmist ultimately do with shame? What can you do? The psalmist takes inventory of his shame and keeps turning it into prayer.

Everything you experience in life has already been prayed in the psalms. Remarkably, God hears and answers your prayers now in ways David himself couldn't have imagined. What do I mean? Jesus Christ was sent to experience all that David suffered. He was wrecked by shame. He was stripped, spat upon, humiliated, and publicly ridiculed. Remarkably, when Jesus was crucified on the cross, he prayed David's words from Psalm 31:5, "Father, into your hands I commit my spirit" (Luke 23:46). If Jesus prayed the psalms in his darkest hour, so should we.

When you struggle with shame, pray as David did:

But I trust in you, O LORD;
>> I say, "You are my God."

My times are in your hand;

> rescue me from the hand of my enemies and from my
> persecutors!

Make your face shine on your servant;

> save me in your steadfast love! (Ps. 31:14–16)

As the God of the Bible rescued David from his enemies, God provides unassailable refuge in the broken and resurrected body of Jesus. Look at Jesus who lost his Father's face at the cross, to ensure the face of God shines on you even if every other face turns away.

Look to Jesus forsaken to make Psalm 27:10 come true for you: "For my father and my mother have forsaken me, but the LORD will take me in."

Look to Jesus: "who for the joy that was set before him endured the cross, despising the shame" (Heb. 12:2), so that he would never be ashamed of you.

In September 2023, I read about the passing of Dr. Sang Hyun Lee, the pioneer of Asian American theology and professor at Princeton Theological Seminary. My first thought was a memory of a remark he made after class: "God loves you in your own skin. You don't have to be more of anything." Dr. Lee articulated the gospel in a way I didn't even know I needed. Jesus is more than enough, in my place. His love casts out all fear (1 John 4:18) and heals all shame.

Your shame doesn't inhibit God's love for you—it ignites his love for you. Shame makes you run and hide like Adam and Eve, but Jesus brings you into the light of confession by running after you. Call upon Jesus to find "hope does not put us to shame, because God's love has been poured into our hearts through the Holy Spirit who has been given to us" (Rom. 5:5).

What does the Asian American church offer to shame sufferers? We display the distinctive power and beauty of the gospel, which is a refuge from shame. Additionally, the Asian American church offers the embodied experience of admitting our shame to one another in an environment of grace. These things—the gospel and Christian community—sustain us until we're home, where shame will be silenced forever.

14

Called to Lead: A Woman's Path
to Church Leadership

by Heidi Wong

Doing full-time ministry as a woman in the Asian American context can be extremely lonely. While your brothers on staff have each other and their larger circle of pastor friends to commiserate and celebrate with, you may not know where to turn. *Am I the only one who feels this way?*

This first part of this chapter is a compilation of moments that led to an unlikely place of leadership within a local Asian American church. The second part includes practical applications for you and the pastoral leaders who labor alongside you for his kingdom. The goal is to spark discussion that will lead to you living the next chapter.

How Did I Get Here?

It was during college at a Korean American campus church that I had my first impactful experience of Christian community. This time of spiritual enrichment coincided with learning to appreciate my multicultural background as a gift rather than the "not enough-ness" I felt growing up. When your last name is Chinese, the Koreans will still consider you as "other," and when you struggle to speak Mandarin, the Chinese will dismiss you as not one of their own. But to White people, you will represent a caricature of Asian defined by movies and media. Learning how to navigate this neither-here-nor-there space provided a certain depth of perspective. It also made Christ's claim on my life that much more meaningful—even if I didn't truly belong anywhere, I had a seat at his table.

I developed a friendship with my college pastor's wife, who was seminary trained. She taught me how to read the Word and ask deep questions. Strengthening the muscle to read analytically made the Bible and other books more accessible. She treated us as people with unique personalities and histories, meeting us where we were but challenging us to go further. In her, I saw a faithful disciple who did not need to abandon her gifts to bless others, and I wanted to one day emulate her.

After I moved to New York, I visited a dozen churches before landing at Exilic, a brand-new church plant. Eventually a few friends from Exilic and I took part in a local program aimed at developing young leaders in the church. How can you discern your calling? What does a gospel movement look like in your community? These discussions made me hungry to learn more, so I decided to enroll in seminary. The senior pastor, Aaron Chung, suggested I join Exilic's staff part-time to help launch the college ministry in addition to receiving oversight as I progressed through the program at Reformed Theological Seminary NYC.

About halfway through school, I began to express frustration. Part of it stemmed from being a part-timer, but a larger part of it was from a lack of clarity. I wanted the pastoral staff to give clear directives on what I could or couldn't do as a woman so I could respect the bounds and not waste my time. When I heard things like, "I'm not sure where I land on that yet," I agonized over having to continue staggering through no-man's-land. I did not want to leave Exilic, but I wasn't sure there was a place for me.

My pastors handled these conversations with grace. In addition to my angst, they were also managing the litany of challenges that come with pastoring. They hadn't dealt with someone like me before—a woman with theological training, open to teaching, with experience in the corporate world—and were in their own learning process. I appreciated their willingness to listen, despite not having immediate answers. This back and forth, though frustrating at times, helped us inch our way toward clarity.

It wasn't an easy decision, but eventually I left my corporate job to join Exilic full time. Since then, I've experienced a deeper appreciation for our staff as we work together for the Great Commission. Doing ministry as a team pushes us to consider new perspectives and humbles us as we hear and speak God's prophetic word to one another.

As you consider your own place in ministry, I offer a few reflections from my hard-earned learning.

Observe Polity and Culture

Understanding your church's polity (the way it is governed) will help you envision a future for yourself. Serving in a lay capacity first provides time for observation. What are your church's mechanisms for accountability? Are decisions made by the vote of members, a group of elders, or just the senior pastor? Wrestling with what you find will force you to grapple with what, according to Scripture, you believe and will submit to. Having conversations with those you trust will sharpen your own theological understanding.

In addition to polity, get a sense of your church's culture. Is unquestioning deference to a specific demographic a norm? Can people vehemently disagree about certain issues and still be united on primary ones? Such observations will help you know what you are stepping into. No church is perfect. Being prepared to gracefully handle its imperfections can mitigate a mismatch in expectations.

To My Sisters

Your brothers on staff, however well-intentioned they may be, will likely say or do things that unnecessarily exclude you. Here are some things to remember as you navigate your own ministry context.

1. Cry Out to the God Who Sees You

Isolation is unhealthy, but a taste of it can force us to cry out to God. The Egyptian Hagar, arguably the loneliest and most invisible woman in Scripture, is given credit as the first person to name God (Gen. 16:13). God saw her need and provided for her.

2. Embrace Your Role as the "Ezer"

To be an effective Ezer, ready for battle alongside your brothers, communication is key. If they don't initiate, invite your pastoral staff to help establish avenues for communication about your experience. They need to grow as shepherds and overseers in addition to caring for you. If you remain silent, they may remain blind to their own deficiencies. God has given you a voice with which to bless the church. Don't be afraid to use it.

3. Develop Deep Friendships

A band of faithful brothers and sisters makes the journey of life easier to endure. This is especially true in ministry. Develop deep friendships with people who know how to support you. Look for friends who will rebuke you when needed as well as embolden you to stand your ground. Having even just one of these close friends provides perspective through the various joys and sorrows of ministry. These kinds of friendships don't develop overnight; you must intentionally seek them out and develop them.

4. Manage Expectations, Trust God

You may be tempted to air your grievances with regard to your church's flaws. Resist this temptation and instead practice patience while listening and observing. Expect that everything will largely remain the same even after you join. If you see yourself as the sole changemaker, you will quickly burn out. Pray with great expectation and invite the Spirit to move among your staff, including in your own heart. As you feel led, share your thoughts with other leaders and learn respectful disagreement.

To My Brothers

Women with leadership qualities may not be able to see a place for themselves in the local church for a variety of reasons. You will have to come alongside the other leaders in your church to provide a vision for what this could look like, even when you don't fully know. Be open to having ongoing conversations for the purpose of landing on something concrete.

This section is organized around a few ideas that are meant to spark thoughts and discussion among your staff.

1. Shepherd Your Whole Staff

In addition to hiring, be thoughtful about how you plan to mentor women on staff. How will they grow, not only in faith but also in their roles in serving the church? Growth and development are baked into a company's culture, however good or bad the program may be. In the church, this may look different. For example, you have probably benefited from informal mentorship and guidance from other pastors in areas like preaching, counseling, and general day-to-day ministry. For you, it may have been organic. A sister who has previously worked in the marketplace will be looking for an avenue for development. It will not come organically simply due to the nature of her role's difference from yours. It's not your responsibility to provide the perfect setup, but it *is* your responsibility to provide this avenue of care. Ask your network of pastors if there are women on their staff who are open to connecting with women you serve with.

Although Christ is our ultimate advocate, as a shepherd you have the responsibility to advocate for the women you work with. Will you put your relational capital with beloved church members on the line for the sake of protecting a female staff member from undue criticism? Will you go out of your way to defend her, even if it means upsetting some of your close brothers?

2. Provide Clarity

Church leadership should strive to be as clear as possible about the roles and bounds of unordained staff. Otherwise, women will waste energy and time hesitantly approaching some invisible edge. If the bounds appear to constantly change or differ by person, then a disorientating cognitive dissonance settles in, and the individual is discouraged from even trying. She will remain in the middle, afraid to make a mistake. This is bad for her and for the church, who will not benefit from the full use of her gifts.

Will it be hard work to provide clarity and wisely navigate difficult conversations? Yes. Might you strongly disagree with other elders or staff with regard to interpretation of Scripture? Yes. However, without this kind of investment there will be no return.

3. See Admin as a Way to Love Others

You have probably preached a sermon about Genesis 1 and the days of creation. You delight when people recognize God's creativity and intentionality. *He brought chaos to order!* In a similar way, you can view your administrative efforts as a way to love others.

Most non-ministry jobs require a basic level of adherence to some kind of structure—whether you're a barista, bartender, or office worker. I encourage those seeking to be in the pastorate to work in a non-ministry job for at least one year. This will enhance your preaching and familiarize you with the everyday vocabulary of your congregation. As you work under a supervisor, you will gain a better understanding of why systems exist and how they help employees flourish. Then you can apply all that learning to your own leadership in ministry.

4. Seek to Include Others

What kind of staff culture do you have? Do you and the boys hang out over golf and cigars? Do you walk into work the morning after a devastating NBA loss and bemoan your dropped fantasy ranking for thirty minutes with another pastor? For you, this kind of culture may be wonderful, allowing you to share and enjoy your passions. Now consider a female staff member who relishes none of the above. How inclusive are you when she's around? Are you able to have enriching theological discussions with her and be sharpened by her perspective?

It's okay for the relationship you have with your male and female staff to be different. But if you feel that one is life-giving while the other is a mere formality, something may be off.

Side by Side

While serving in the Asian American church as a woman can present challenges, working together with others for the gospel adds color to the great partnerships in Scripture. Esther wouldn't have made it without Mordecai's encouragement. The church in Rome may have never received what we now refer to as the book of Romans without the friendship between Phoebe and Paul (Rom. 16:1). As you prayerfully continue on this journey, know that arriving at a healthy dynamic takes time. Ambiguity is often an opportunity to grow, and having a team of sisters and brothers who can share that journey together with you can be a great blessing to you and the church that you serve. May you be encouraged to go where God calls you, remembering that he has gone before you.

15

Steadfast: Persevering Through Difficult Seasons of Ministry

by Joey Chen

If you've been in ministry longer than a few months, it is likely you've thought about leaving your church or quitting ministry. If you were leading during the COVID pandemic, that question probably came up regularly in your prayers. Recent statistics reveal that 41 percent of pastors have considered quitting ministry in the last twelve months.[46]

You are not alone. The first time I wanted to give up came when almost all the volunteers quit during my first month of youth ministry. I inherited a volunteer team that faithfully served for a year without a youth pastor. I learned the hard way that volunteers are often more relationally committed to people than the mission. Their quick departure was emotionally devastating.

I also walked into a staff conflict that would cause all senior leaders to leave within that first year. The result was a church with no senior staff that was hurting and in need of care. To complicate things, I had moved across the country for this position—a decision I questioned amid so much uncertainty.

I've now been a pastor for sixteen years in the same Chinese heritage church. I have struggled through many challenging seasons. This chapter is for the leader wrestling with staying and trying to persevere in the Asian American church. If you have difficulty working with the first-generation or established leaders, if you are feeling discouragement from power dynamics of the church, or if you're wrestling with how to leave or when to leave, I want you to know that you're not alone.

As a ministry leader, you're in one of three positions:

1. You are currently going through a difficult season,
2. You are about to go through a difficult season, or
3. You are coming out of a difficult season.

By God's grace, rather than merely surviving difficult seasons, you can learn from them and come out on the other end with greater faith, hope, and love for your church. Let's explore how.

The First Few Years

At an Asian American Youth Ministry Conference in 2005, Pastor Joseph Tsang gave a talk that changed my life. I have no idea what his session was about, but he gave the following advice: "When you first arrive at your church, you should commit to staying at least five years because in the first five years you're building trust and credibility. If you don't fail or get fired, do your best to stay no matter how difficult the ministry."

Those words became a lifesaver as I came into a major crisis within the first years of ministry. Many people experience a honeymoon period when they get to a church—a time when the blemishes and problems haven't surfaced yet. There is an abundance of patience and courtesy regarding differences. However, if you serve in an Asian American church, it is likely you had little to no honeymoon.

One of the greatest challenges is often *established culture*. The established culture is not always obvious. It's the unstated values that shape the church. Culture is usually not defined in the church's doctrinal statement. It's the implicit theology that shapes the priorities, decision-making, finances, expectations of how to spend your time, and day-to-day operations.

In Asian American churches, shame is an unspoken—but undeniable—aspect of the established culture. Ben Shin and Sheryl Silzer, in their book, *Tapestry of Grace*, highlight how shame plays a significant role in the culture of our Asian churches. They give the example of couples dealing with marital issues who "rather than asking for help and counsel … often hide the problem and it doesn't surface until divorce papers are served."[47] This kind of hiding sadly describes how some church leaders relate to one another. Although our stated theology may be the good news of Jesus and grace, shame unfortunately permeates the culture.

Established cultures resist change, even small ones. I observed this when a new pastor wanted to challenge the congregation to evangelize more. He gave money to church members to take initiative in personal evangelism efforts. The pastor didn't communicate this new effort with the other leaders and used it as an application of his sermon. If you're cringing, you probably already know what happened. The effort was met with intense criticism because he was introducing a new effort without giving existing leadership a chance to discuss and support the new effort. When members brought questions and criticism to the leadership, their lack of awareness and involvement brought shame.

Every church has established cultural values and expectations regarding new initiatives. Maybe you've done something similar in your church and faced criticism and frustration. Maybe your efforts are necessary and helpful for the church. Many even agree and support the change, yet it fails or is resisted. How do you persevere when the established culture resists your desire to lead or even conflicts with biblical values?

The solution may be found in the concept of honor, which is the antidote to shame. Jayson Georges defines honor this way: "Honor is a person's social worth, one's value in the eyes of the community. Honor is when other people think well of you, resulting in harmonious social bonds in the community. Honor comes from relationships."[48] Jesus takes our shame on the cross and gives us his honor (Eph. 2:4–6), so that the Father looks upon us with love and joy just as he does toward Jesus. Christ honors us by making us co-heirs with him (Rom. 8:16–17) and we are welcomed as adopted children through faith.

Honor provides the perspective and power needed to handle cultural differences. It is easy to focus on the differences as problems that need to be fixed, especially if they are not your cultural values. Honor in practical terms is looking to the interests of others as a priority. In the previous example about launching a new evangelism initiative, the pastor could have had conversations with the other leaders before presenting it to the congregation. Honor involves listening to the ways that the church has *already* pursued evangelism. It includes learning how the church responds to new initiatives and what the standard process is for suggesting them. Honor doesn't mean giving up new initiatives; it means pursuing them while considering their impact on relationships with leaders and the church.

In the early years of ministry, you will face established cultural differences. Rather than seeing everything as a conflict or despairing at the lack of change, think about your life and how God has changed you—how he's *still* changing you. Chances are, it's taken you years, even decades, to become the person God made you to be. You've resisted his work at times, but nonetheless God stayed with you, waited on you, and loved you. I encourage you to remember how Christ has richly honored you and to honor others similarly. In your early years, a posture of honor builds trust for future change.

The Middle Years

In his sermon, Joseph Tsang shared another bit of counsel I've held onto. He said, "After five years of ministry in the same church, evaluate if it's time to stay or go." He then called us to consider staying for another ten years, because that's when changes are possible and ministry fruit often grows. It is in this season where vision can be implemented based on established trust. In these middle years you will have earned some credibility and can begin to tackle culture and begin to press into your vision.

Differences with Established Leadership

Unless you plant a church, you will inherit leadership. It may be elders, deacons, councils, boards, or simply people with significant influence. In Asian American churches, it's often the first generation who are in those positions because they likely started the church. They are likely the official leaders of the church because culture reinforces it through a hierarchy of age. Even those without official positions are often in positions of influence because of cultural values. While not all this is problematic, it is often a challenge to know how to make decisions. It is also a problem if the culture supersedes biblical qualifications. Working with established leaders is one of the most difficult challenges of perseverance.

In Asian American churches, leadership is *hierarchal* and generally *patriarchal* due to its Confucian cultural background. This is "a distinct leadership structure defining who is above whom; that is, those who are younger serve those who are older, and women serve men."[49] This cultural paradigm finds its way into Asian American churches and creates unhealthy leadership, structures, and practices.

In deference to age, character can be overlooked. An overdeveloped reverence for the older generation fails to empower younger, qualified leaders. I've been in one church my entire sixteen years of ministry, and I'm still regularly perceived as the "young pastor." I would encourage you to saturate yourself in 1 Timothy 4:11–15:

> Command and teach these things. Let no one despise you for your youth, but set the believers an example in speech, in conduct, in love, in faith, in purity. Until I come, devote yourself to the public reading of Scripture, to exhortation, to teaching. Do not neglect the gift you have, which was given you by prophecy when the council of elders laid their hands on you. Practice these things, immerse yourself in them, so that all may see your progress.

Paul understood that Timothy would have difficulties with the Ephesian culture and leadership. The way to lead through such difficulties is by being exemplary in life and ministry. It is easy to focus on the people you cannot change while failing to be faithful in the areas you *can* control.

The first five years of my ministry were chaotic due to staff departures. When things are emotionally heated, it is easy to neglect the fundamentals. During those challenging years I focused on what I could do: pray, care for people, try to faithfully preach the word. As I refocused on my life and ministry, the church observed my growth as a preacher and leader. This led me to be the candidate for lead pastor at thirty years old.

Raise Up New Leaders

As you establish trust, it is crucial to bring up new leaders that can both honor the present and help you develop new cultures and initiatives. These change efforts should be biblically anchored and be expressed in contextually wise ways. The goal is not change for the sake of change, nor should it be changed to fit your preferences; any change should always aim toward gospel centrality and biblical faithfulness.

When I became the lead pastor, I focused on correcting the culture of the existing leaders and calling them to embrace new values and vision. This effort was anchored in biblical principles and our commitment to the gospel, so I assumed there would be alignment. In this effort I spent too much attention correcting individuals who I saw were unaligned and ministries that were adrift. Correction is an important part of leading change, but because I only focused on correcting misaligned leaders and ministries, it drained myself and others. I became frustrated when my inherited leaders did not want to change procedures or transform culture.

I needed to identify new leaders to help shift the culture. In addition to the fundamental qualifications of character, it is important that the new leaders are respected by the existing ones and can wisely help move the leadership culture in the direction for the new generation. This means prioritizing relationships. New leaders must be intentional to connect and build trust across the church.

As new leaders are recognized in the church, they will become a source of encouragement and the greatest change agents. Change cannot come from one leader, nor can it come by mere confrontation, so always have an eye for who those leaders are. When you recognize them, be intentional about discipling them.

The Later Years

Few ministry leaders even reach this season. Thom Rainer calls this part of the pastoral cycle a mystery because there is not enough data to determine consistent patterns.[50] If you reach this stage, you have persevered through many seasons. You have resisted the urge to quit, and you have overcome personal and external difficulties. Whether you experience fruitfulness or frustration during this season, you will likely come to ask if it is time to move on. You may have asked yourself this question many times before—sometimes out of frustration, sometimes looking to escape.

In this season, the question of staying or leaving should be stewarded carefully for your ministry and the health of the church. To help proactively address this question, consider these principles.

Question the Status Quo

You're in a good place but aren't adapting or pressing forward in ways the church needs for the next season. Nothing bad occurs, but the church is comfortable because you are comfortable, which leaves it unprepared for new challenges. You're maintaining the status quo, but not reaching new generations or new people who have moved into the area surrounding your church.

For example, consider churches planted in Chinatown. Once thriving in evangelism and community involvement, many of these churches become commuter churches because people become more affluent and move away to areas with better schools. This leaves the church unprepared to reach new generations, because fewer congregants live in the neighborhood and share common experiences with those in the community.

Leaders need to steward this question of staying or going, not just for themselves, but also to help the church address its own need to change for the future. Wrestling with this question is necessary for the church to adapt to new seasons. When leaders commit with renewed vision, it pushes the church to stretch and grow.

Articulate Your Vision for the Future

When I approached fifteen years at my church, I knew it was time to evaluate my vision for the future and my role in the church. I didn't want to become stagnant in my leadership, and I didn't want the church to become comfortable around me. If you have been in your church for more than ten years, the church trusts you and is willing to follow your leadership, even if you end up being stuck in your vision and leadership. It's tempting to not want to rock the boat and slip into maintenance mode. This is especially true in Asian American churches, where confronting leaders and having difficult conversations is often avoided.

As I evaluated myself and the church, I saw the need for changes to pursue the vision I had for the future of the church. Self-evaluation is a humbling process that requires you to invite people to speak honestly into your life and ministry. Rarely is this initiated by others in the Asian American church because criticism is shameful. However, hearing different perspectives about your life, ministry, and dreams is important for personal growth. I did this by inviting fourteen leaders to pray with me and ask questions about me personally and about my vision. This included pastors and non-pastors who I trust from different seasons in my life. Their prayer, conversation, and support were crucial to my discernment process. If you find yourself asking if you should stay or leave, seek wise counsel.

I know there are various opinions about how transparent to be when considering plans that include the possibility of leaving, but if there is trust and mutual love, I believe it's best to share with leaders. God used this time of openness and vulnerability to clarify my own calling and help the church wrestle with important changes for the next season.

Having a sounding board of people who are familiar and unfamiliar with the church was helpful to highlight the main issues. I was able to identify that the barriers were not theological or foundational, but organizational and cultural. I shared the ideas with the leadership, hoping that they would consider them earnestly. I expected hesitation but hoped that there would be openness to discussion. As expected, it was met with a mix of defensiveness, fear, resistance, and an earnest desire for change.

The next eighteen months were full of hard conversations. There were many disappointments, and I had to hold the changes with an open hand before the Lord. I also believed that I needed to be open with my calling to the church. I was convicted that changes were crucial for the next season, but I also knew that I could not force changes on the church. This tension could mean that my time at the church was completed, so I opened myself up to a few opportunities.

In the end, God moved the leaders of my church to embrace the changes, and he closed a door to another opportunity. Articulating your vision can be risky, since it can be rejected, but it's the only way to provide clarity for yourself and those you serve. It sparks important conversations that can be difficult, but they are vital for the future of the church.

Be a Blessing

No matter what season you find yourself in currently, don't let the hardships define you. The writer of Hebrews 12:2 tells us that Jesus endured the cross because of "the joy that was set before him." You are part of that joy. You are a beloved child of God before you are a leader.

One of my friends told me that when I chose to stay, it meant a lot to him. We are not in the same church, so I did not think much of it. But upon reflection, I realized how God uses the endurance of one person to spur someone else to grow and endure in faith.

Joseph Tsang didn't give advice for the years beyond fifteen years, so here's my advice for those who continue to endure in ministry. Make it a priority to bear the burdens of others who are struggling to endure. Do this inside and outside your church. Schedule time in your rhythms to be a blessing to other pastors, especially new pastors in your area. Buy them lunch, write them an encouraging letter, call them and offer to pray for their family and ministry, babysit their kids, or guest preach to give them a break. Buy coffee for the college student in your church who's wrestling with their faith.

If you have persevered through difficult seasons of ministry, you can be a powerful encouragement to those who are struggling. Jesus will use your perseverance for his glory and the building of his church.

16

FOBO in Ministry: Navigating the Temptation of Greener Pastures in Ministry

by David Larry Kim

It was my last semester of seminary, and for the past year I had been thinking and praying about what to do after graduating. For three and a half years I had served as the youth pastor at a small Korean immigrant church in Orlando. I had come to Orlando for seminary, drawn to the small Korean community there, but I knew no one. I wanted to learn how to love and shepherd a group of people, to preach the Word, and to build a gospel foundation where not many had labored before. After four years, I expected to move on. The church offered me the position of English Congregation pastor, and while it was very appealing to me, it didn't seem to fit with the path that others had advised me to take.

Have you ever been in that place? Wondering whether you should stay or go? Maybe your situation was different, but if you've been there, you know the struggle is real. Perhaps you're in that place now.

Bigger is Better! Right?

After months of fasting and praying, I still didn't have clarity except for the near-universal advice I'd received from friends, mentors, professors, and pastors:

- You should leave Orlando.
- You must go to a big city.
- Go somewhere with a lot of Asians.
- Get experience at a big church with a lot of resources.
- Get your name out there.

It made sense. Make the biggest impact. Maximize my potential. Broaden my influence. With that advice in mind, I applied to positions in cities like Los Angeles, Chicago, Atlanta, and Asian American hubs like New Jersey and Virginia. Staying at my church certainly had its appeal, but I didn't want to base my decision on how I felt about the people. So as graduation got closer, I decided to tell my church I would be moving on. I didn't know where I would end up, but I felt I owed it to them to give them time to find a pastor.

The Morning That Changed My Life

I requested a meeting with my senior pastor after worship services one Sunday afternoon. The day before, I wanted to spend some time in prayer to surrender this decision to God. I went to Saturday morning prayer and was honest with God. "God, I don't know where I'm supposed to go. It's going to be hard to leave my people, but please guide me. Would you speak to my heart?" As I waited in silence, three things happened.

The best way to describe the first is to say it was like the Microsoft Windows screensavers of the 1990s. Do you remember the one where the Windows logos were flying through space? In my mind's eye, instead of Windows, I saw faces of people in Orlando, people in my church, who I'd grown to love deeply over the past few years.

Second, the Lord spoke Matthew 9:36–38 into my heart:

> When he saw the crowds, he had compassion for them, because they were harassed and helpless, like sheep without a shepherd. Then he said to his disciples, "The harvest is plentiful, but the laborers are few; therefore pray earnestly to the Lord of the harvest to send out laborers into his harvest."

Third, I remembered the words that a Korean pastor said to me when I first arrived in Orlando: "No pastor has stayed at a Korean church in Orlando for more than five years. Most leave after three. And that's the Korean side. There has only been one full-time English Ministry (EM) pastor in Orlando. When things get hard, they leave for greener pastures and bigger cities. Church members here don't know what it is to persevere because their pastors have not shown them."

In that moment, my heart began to break for the English-speaking sheep in Orlando who had never had a shepherd walk with them. I wrestled with God, saying, "I made up my mind to leave but now you're confusing me. It feels like you're telling me to stay." Have you ever felt like God was messing with your plans?

Sure enough, at that very moment, God was divinely orchestrating other events to make it clear that he was calling me to be the shepherd of the church here in Orlando. This was my Macedonian Call.

The next day, I told my senior pastor and other church leaders that I would stay and accept the call to be the EM pastor. Much has changed over the last nineteen years, but one thing is clear: I am where God wants me to be, and my heart for my church has never been fuller.

Greener Pastures and Bigger Cities

Through the years, there have been opportunities to go to greener pastures and bigger cities. There have been offers for positions of greater influence, and I have been tempted to leave. I know I'm not alone. The owners of the Korean American Ministry Resources website have said that their site gets more hits from pastors looking for new positions on Sunday night than at any other time.[51] Ministry wanderlust is a real thing. Have you ever felt it? Have you ever been curious to know if there was a better ministry position out there for you?

Nineteen years have passed, and I have not left my church. For me, the reason is simple: God has called me here and until He releases me from the call, I want to be faithful. Unless the Lord says that my time here is done, this is the best place for me. Do you trust that the same is true for you? If God has called you somewhere, take heart and stay where he's planted you. There will always be more appealing positions than your present situation. But leaving before God's appointed time would mean forsaking the call. In my own life and ministry, I've seen God honor my decision to stay in many ways.

FOBO, Not FOMO

It's not hard to find pastors who are unhappy where they are. I've heard it said, "It's not FOMO (fear of missing out) but FOBO (fear of better options)." But how do you define *better*? What does that mean to you? Is it defined by size? Salary? What if God's measure of success isn't the same as ours? What if God sees things differently than the world? What if Jesus is teaching us something by shunning crowds for small towns and leaving the ninety-nine for the one? Jesus certainly wasn't saying that bigger is always bad. Ultimately, it isn't about the size and scope of the ministry. It is about being faithful with what he has entrusted to us.

Ministry is a calling to be obeyed, not just a career to be advanced. I wonder how many pastors have left their churches a bit too early, due to frustration, a better situation, or some other reason. What if God was calling them to persevere a little bit longer? What if the sweetest fruits of faithfulness were waiting right around the corner? Let's be faithful where God has placed us, until he tells us that our time is done.

The Sweet Fruit of Faithfulness

I've heard preachers use the Chinese bamboo tree as an illustration. Once it's planted, it needs to be watered and tended to regularly, even though there's no visible fruit for the first four years. But in the fifth year, the tree grows ninety feet in five weeks. Sometimes you can't see fruit unless you've been faithful for a few years. As I reflect on the past twenty-two years at my church, I have seen many fruits of faithfulness. Some are obvious: Your people become your family. You develop gravitas. You get to see long-prayed prayers answered. Babies grow up to be co-laborers, then get sent into the mission field. You have the best seats in the house for weddings, baptisms, and other celebrations. You have the privilege of walking with people in loss. But there are also deeper, hidden fruits of remaining faithful in the Asian American church where God has called you to be. Here are just a few.

Clarity

Have you ever been at one job, while interviewing for other ones? Didn't it feel kind of like you were cheating on a loved one? There was exactly one time in my ministry career where I was praying about another pastoral position, and that's what it felt like. When I'm faithful to where God has called me, I am fully present instead of thinking about what opportunities might await or where the next season will take me. My focus becomes clear.

This is especially helpful when times get hard. Clarity allows me to devote myself to being the best shepherd that I can be to the sheep entrusted to me, rather than wondering if sheep in other pastures might like me better or appreciate me more. Instead of tolerating people or thinking about loving them in theory, I can get down to the business of actually loving the real people I'm called to serve. Do you ever feel unable to love your people fully because your thoughts wander to where else you could be serving?

Self-Awareness

When you are in a healthy environment where both grace and truth are embodied, you will begin to see your strengths and weaknesses. About ten years ago, I was part of a pastoral cohort that delved deeply into our personal lives. One of the requirements for the cohort was you had to have served at the same church for at least five years. Many pastors can get by on their strengths, gifts, and personality for a few years. But if you're with a group of people long enough, you will see weaknesses that you are tempted to ignore and unhealthy patterns that you are tempted to excuse—but you can't. The longer you stay, the clearer the mirror that reveals your true self.

Through the cohort, I recognized a pattern in myself: I was unwilling to get angry at people. If someone would come late to a meeting, I would dismiss it, choosing to "extend grace" and forgive quickly. But after years of doing this, what I thought was a sign of health and maturity was really an unwillingness to engage in hard conversations. I would rather let people off the hook than risk offending them. Realizing this allowed me to engage with my emotions in healthier ways and to express them in ways that led to relational depth. Have you seen the fruit of self-awareness grow in your life?

Mutual Honor

How do you feel when you think about the first-generation immigrant church? For many people, the thought can be triggering. My church, Harvest, resides on the same campus as the Korean church that birthed us (Vision Church). Although it isn't always easy, our relationship has been a mutual blessing, marked by mutual trust, vision, and sacrifice forged through time. Without a relationship with someone, we fall back on stereotypes. In the Korean church, it's said that the KM (Korean Ministry) stands for "Killing Ministry" and EM (English Ministry) stands for "Easy Ministry." The first-gen church caricatures the second-gen as lazy. The second-gen caricatures the first-gen as crazy!

But a funny thing happens when you stick it out and strive for unity. Those stereotypes began to change. Vision Church and their leadership has always said that the thriving of Harvest Church is more important than their own survival. Time and again, they have put that thought into action. In our early days, when space was limited, their congregation of 250 would switch sanctuaries with our 120-members congregation on Easter Sunday. They would cram into our 160-seat sanctuary so that we and our guests could worship in the 700-seat sanctuary. By inconveniencing themselves, our guests could be comfortable. When we worship together, they allow Harvest to lead worship and preach, so younger, English-speaking generations can understand. They approved of a higher salary for me, acknowledging my personal needs and stage of life. We have learned and been blessed so much from the Korean church.

Beautifully, the blessing has gone both ways. The Korean church has learned from us about grace, rest, emotional health, the gospel, and contextualization. What are some ways that you have been blessed by the immigrant church? And what are the gifts that you have given to them? By sticking around for years—what Eugene Peterson calls "a long obedience in the same direction"[52]—you can build trust with those you serve.

A Stunning Vision of God's Family

By remaining in my present situation, through the ups and downs, I've witnessed the intergenerational beauty the immigrant church is meant to embody. Part of that was through my former senior pastor, Inki Kim. When I was going through ordination, our presbytery's examining committee asked him how he was going to mitigate against the all-too-familiar tale of immigrant churches experiencing generational conflict. I wasn't present, but two of my church members said that Pastor Inki paused for a moment before saying through tears, "David is like my son. I would never do anything to hurt him. I want nothing more than for him to succeed, even more than I want my congregation to succeed." He has demonstrated this time and time again. In many ways, he was like a father to me. Through his example, I want to become that kind of a father figure to people in my church. Over the years, former students have gone on to pastoral ministry and into the mission field. Several have served with me on our staff. What a joy to see former students and "children" become co-laborers. In the same way that Pastor Inki dreamed for me, my dream is for my ceiling to be their floor.

God Honors Faithfulness

Jesus said that if you are faithful with little, he will entrust you with more (e.g., Matt. 25:21–23). God honors faithfulness with greater opportunities, but it will not look the same with everyone. Opportunities come in unexpected ways. Moses went from herding sheep to shepherding people through the wilderness. David went from fighting off animals to slaying giants. Joseph went from Potiphar's assistant to prime minister of Egypt. John went from caring for Jesus's mother to penning Scripture. The point is, though the journey looks different for everyone, God honors faithfulness.

How has God honored faithfulness in your life? How does that inspire you to be faithful to what God has placed in front of you? Faithfulness may not always lead to a larger platform or bigger ministry. Some people never move beyond their present situations. But the faithful are able to experience the ripe fruit of God's favor in their obedience, and they have the promise of much more in the life to come. May we do our part in being faithful and trust God to be faithful to his promises.

I'm the Man and I'm Gonna Kick Butt

At the top of every sermon manuscript, I type a few phrases that remind me of my call to shepherd my people. One of these phrases says, "I'm the man and I'm gonna kick butt." I don't write that to boast or to boost my ego. I write it as a reminder of my calling—God has called *me* to feed *my* sheep on any given Sunday morning. At a broader level, he's called me to lead my flock during this season of my church's life. He hasn't called anyone else to shepherd Harvest Church—not Francis Chan, not Tim Keller, not [insert famous preacher]. He has called *me* to this. He chose me and because of that, in this season, I'm his man and I'm gonna kick butt.

And that's true of you also. Wherever God has you, you are the person that he has called for this season. So be faithful for as long as God has you there. What might that look like in your present situation?

Where Are You Now?

How does this apply to where you are now? Does frustration with your church or with the immigrant church make you want to leave?

Have you grown weary in your present situation? Are you on the verge of leaving?

Before you do, can I encourage you to take some time to pray again? I know you have been praying, but pray with others. Wait on God. Seek godly wisdom. Solicit counsel from those you love and trust and who know you well. God may indeed be releasing you from your call, and the burden for your people may be lifted and given to another. It may also be that God wants you to stay a bit longer. To persevere for the sake of your growth and the maturing of your people. Some of your most glorious ministry moments may be on the other side of just a little bit more faithfulness. Difficulties don't always signal that your time is done.

The Perfect Embodiment

The Bible is full of examples of people who remained faithful to their calling amid challenges. None stand taller than Jesus. He knew His calling clearly. Perhaps the temptation of greener grass was never stronger than when he prayed in the garden, begging the Father to take the cup from him. He knew the price of faithfulness. He knew it would cost everything. Yet, he chose to obey the Father: "Nevertheless, not my will, but yours, be done" (Luke 22:42). He did that for you. He did that for me. He did that for the glory of his Father.

- Jesus rejected greener pastures to embrace his calling.
- He rejected the positions, passions, and possessions with which the devil tempted him to embrace his Father's plan.
- He left heaven to come to earth.
- He rejected comfort for the cross.
- He chose to save us over himself.
- Above all, He chose to be faithful.

That is what God calls us to be as well.

One day, we will stand before our Savior. It will be the joy of joys when we stand before our Savior and he speaks over us those words that we have so desperately longed to hear: not "Well done, my good and *famous* servant," not "Well done, my good and *fruitful* servant," but "Well done, [my] good and *faithful* servant" (Matt. 25:21).

May this be true of us.

Conclusion

The Future of the Asian American Church

by Steve S. Chang

As we put this book together, a few prominent themes became evident.

First, **there is great value and opportunity in the Asian Immigrant Church**. Faith Chang began with the question, "Why does our church even exist?" She answered by reminding us of the beauty and opportunity in in the Asian immigrant church. Others wrote of the unique values that one can find in the immigrant church through its diversity (Enoch Y. Liao), multilingual services (Jason M. Tarn), unique ministry opportunities (Monica M. Kim), and intergenerational mentorship (Michael Lee). Instead of seeing the immigrant church as a place to leave, many saw it as a place in which to find beauty and flourish.

Second, **there is legitimacy, theology, and calling for the Asian American Church**. Owen Y. Lee wrote of the burden that many Asian American leaders feel to become multiethnic and how it's possible to thank God for the church he's called you to. Aaron J. Chung explained how Asian American churches create safe havens for those living in exile.

Third, **churches must contextualize ministry to the Asian American faith community.** Instead of muting our culture, several of our authors wrote about how to contextualize ministry for Asian Americans through preaching (Hanley Liu) and ministry to singles (Soojin Park). We also learned about the legacy of Cory K. Ishida who contextualized ministry for more than forty decades. We believe that practical theology for ministering in the Asian American church is woefully underdeveloped. What does it mean to do ministry for Asian Americans? This question cannot be answered by academics alone but by practitioners in the trenches. By developing our own voice and ecclesiology as exilic minority communities, we believe we can help reverse the dechurching trend among younger Asian Americans. We believe this is something that should be studied and written about in years to come.

Fourth, **Asian American church leaders face unique internal and external challenges.** Asian American church leaders have to wrestle with proving themselves worthy through success. It is a part of our works-oriented Asian culture and our survival as minorities and immigrants. Harold Y. Kim aptly confessed, "I was terrified of failing at something I gave myself to." Heidi Wong wrote of being a woman leader in a male-dominant church space. Joey Chen wrote of trying to work through various seasons of leadership in the Chinese heritage church. David Larry Kim wrote of his struggle with fear of better options (FOBO). Kim N. Kira reminded us that the gospel must cut through the idols and pains of our heart.

Fifth, **there is a great opportunity and calling for Asian American leaders to minister to the emerging generations in the Asian**

Immigrant church, the third-culture Asian American church, and the majority-culture/multiethnic church. This book is meant to sound the horn about the emerging generation of Asian Americans leaving the church en masse. Our prayer is that this book helps the elders of this generation accept the responsibility to reverse this trend. We must worry less about who we are not and steward who we are and the generation coming after us. There is no single solution, but we must do our part within the immigrant church and third-culture churches to reach the emerging generation where they are.

We are also very aware that Asian Americans encompass more than Koreans, Chinese, and Japanese. We believe there will be greater collaboration among Asian American churches and leaders, especially those of non-East-Asian descent. We observe that third- and fourth-generation Asian Americans will lean toward racialized multiculturalism and believe churches will follow suit. We cannot elevate one path while diminishing others. We need to encourage all types of work for the glory of God and the salvation of many.

TERMINOLOGY

Asian American (sometimes hyphenated) describes a person of Asian descent living in the United States. Those who are of East Asian, Southeast Asian, South Asian, Central Asian, and Western Asian descent can all be identified as Asian Americans (although not all self-identify in the same way). The term can also encompass those who are Pacific Islanders, adoptees, mixed race, or in the country temporarily. In most cases, the authors also are speaking about those of Asian descent who are in Western countries such as Canada, England, and Australia.

Asian American church refers to a church whose makeup is majority Asian American, whether it is expressly Asian American or not. Sociologists would say that the church must be more than 80 percent Asian American to be classified in this way, but most of our authors were not precise in this way. Also, *Pan-Asian church, Multi-Asian church, Asian American church.*

Asian immigrant church refers to a church with an Asian heritage history, composition, and language services. These churches are dominated by recent immigrants from Asia and conduct services in their native language. It can refer to a Chinese immigrant church with services in Cantonese, Mandarin, and English; a Korean immigrant church with services in Korean and English; or any other immigrant church with services in the native language. Also, *Asian American immigrant church, Asian immigrant American church, immigrant church.*

Chinese/Korean/Japanese Immigrant Church refers to an immigrant church from a specific ethnic heritage. Also, *Chinese/Korean/Japanese immigrant church, Chinese/Korean/Japanese church,*

Chinese/Korean/Japanese Heritage church.

Chinese American, Japanese American, Korean American (sometimes hyphenated) refer to individuals who live in the United States who are of a specific Asian descent. Our contributors used these ethnic labels to refer to ethnicity, not nationality. For example, our contributors often speak of Chinese Americans who not only trace their heritage from the People's Republic of China, but also those who are ethnically Chinese but come from Taiwan, Hong Kong, Singapore, or elsewhere.

First-generation, 1.5-generation, second-generation refer to one's distance from their immigration history. A first-generation immigrant is someone who was born outside of the United States and is currently living in the United States. Individuals who came to the United States as children are 1.5-generation immigrants. The second-generation was born in the United States to parents who are first-generation immigrants.

Majority culture refers to the dominant, mostly White, culture in the United States. This is a sociological term used loosely in this book. Also, *dominant culture.*

Multiethnic church refers to a church that does not have one dominant (80 percent) ethnic group. Technically speaking, an Asian American church with no dominant ethnic group (e.g., Chinese American) can be considered multiethnic. Some may use the term multiethnic church to refer to a multiracial church, where there is no dominant racial (e.g., White or Black) group.

Third-culture refers to the culture that is neither majority culture nor immigrant culture. It is a term often undefined, changing, and transitional.

CONTRIBUTORS

Faith Chang (BS Cornell University; Certificate in Christian Studies, Westminster Theological Seminary) serves at Grace Christian Church on Staten Island where her husband is a pastor. She is the author of *Peace over Perfection: Enjoying A Good God When You Feel You're Never Good Enough* and cohost of the Westminster Kids Digest Podcast at the Westminster Bookstore. She enjoys writing on theology, ministry, and the Christian life.

Steve S. Chang was born in Korea and immigrated to Los Angeles at the age of nine in 1971. He studied computer engineering at UCLA and worked in the industry before going to Dallas Theological Seminary (ThM). Steve founded Living Hope Community Church (Brea, California) and has been serving as the senior pastor for more than thirty years. Steve and his wife, Hannah, have two married children, Christine and Janice, and enjoy grandparenting Evan and Titus. Steve also has his DMin from Talbot School of Theology and cofounded SOLA Network.

Joey Chen serves as lead English pastor of Sunset Church in San Francisco. He responded to a calling to ministry in his senior year of high school and went on to Cedarville University and Trinity Evangelical Divinity School (MDiv). He has served at Sunset Church for sixteen years, starting as the youth pastor in 2007 and then becoming the lead English pastor in 2012. He received his DMin from Talbot School of Theology in church multiplication and is committed to missional work by serving on the board of OMF US and Stratum, a Bay Area church-planting incubator. He is married to Jeannette and is blessed with their two girls, Melia and Selah.

Aaron J. Chung is the founder and senior pastor of Exilic in New York City. He is a graduate of Westminster Seminary California (MDiv) and Westminster Theological Seminary (DMin). He guest lectures at Reformed Theological Seminary NYC and is a council member of the SOLA Network. He has written on a variety of subjects—from theology to sports—for media outlets like *Relevant Magazine* and *The Bleacher Report*. He is married to Hanna and is a girl dad to Logan and Hayden. They live in Manhattan and love doing life there.

Cory K. Ishida was born in Alhambra, California, in 1947. He grew up in Pasadena, California, and graduated from UCLA as a pre-med major. Cory was married in 1969 to his wife, Reine. They have three daughters and thirteen grandchildren ages five to twenty-three. He was called into ministry in 1972 and worked as a pharmaceutical representative for five years before accepting the senior pastor position at Evergreen Baptist Church in 1977. While serving, he completed his seminary education at Fuller Theological Seminary. Cory pastored Evergreen Los Angeles for twenty years. He planted Evergreen San Gabriel Valley in 1997 and served for twenty-two years before retiring in 2019.

David Larry Kim is married to Olivia and is the proud father of Emmanuelle, Elijah, and Elyse. He is the lead pastor of Harvest Church, an intergenerational congregation of house churches that was planted by the Korean Presbyterian Church of Orlando. He has served at Harvest since 2001. David grew up in Virginia, graduated from the University of Virginia and Reformed Theological Seminary, and serves on the Council of SOLA Network. He is passionate about communicating the truth of God's Word and enjoys playing and watching sports. Before podcasts were invented, he cohosted a call-in radio show for teenagers in the Washington, DC, area.

Monica M. Kim (BA University of Toronto; MAR Westminster Theological Seminary; MEd Lehigh University; PhD Lehigh University) is a licensed psychologist who has been counseling for almost twenty years. She has taught counseling courses as an associate faculty member at the Christian Counseling and Educational Foundation (CCEF) and as a lecturer at Westminster Theological Seminary (WTS). She currently serves as an adjunct faculty member at Lehigh University and as a consultant providing counselor training at CCEF. She also has a private practice. Monica is married to Danny Kwon, and they have three adult children, Luke, Noah, and Caleb.

Harold Y. Kim (BA UC Berkeley; MDiv Gordon-Conwell Theological Seminary; ThM Princeton Theological Seminary) is the founding pastor of Christ Central of Southern California since 2007. Harold is married to SunHi and has two daughters, Taylor and Elizabeth. He also serves as President of SOLA Network and Christ Central Network.

Kim N. Kira is the primary teaching elder at Lighthouse Community Church in Torrance, California. He loves being part of a church family that is committed to loving God with all their heart, soul, mind, and strength. Kim is driven by a deep desire to encourage people to experience the transformative power of the gospel. Beyond ministry, Kim loves spending time with his wife Jen and their four children.

Michael Lee serves as the lead pastor of All Nations Community Church. Michael moved from Atlanta to Los Angeles to attend the University of Southern California, majoring in philosophy. After USC, he attended Talbot Theological Seminary and earned his MDiv. Michael also serves as a council member and the executive director of the SOLA Network. He is a huge USC Trojan football fan, avid golfer, and donut aficionado. He and his wife Alice reside in Arcadia with their two children, Seth and Brooke.

Owen Y. Lee has served as the senior pastor of Christ Central Presbyterian Church (Centreville, VA) since 2012. He received his BA in rhetoric from UC Berkeley and his MDiv from Westminster Seminary, California. He is an ordained teaching elder in the Presbyterian Church in America and also serves as the director of operations for the Korean American Leadership Initiative (a ministry of Mission to North America). His purpose and passion are to preach the gospel and to serve the Korean American Church by encouraging and empowering Korean American pastors and leaders. He is married to Margaret, and they have three adult children—Abby, Caleb, and Lizzy.

Enoch Y. Liao serves at Boston Chinese Evangelical Church. He is married to Karen and they have three sons at home and one daughter who has passed on. Enoch received his education from UCLA and Talbot School of Theology. Enoch is also currently enrolled in the PhD program at Western Seminary. He is the author of *In Reverence and Awe*, a practical worship leading resource. He is a cofounder and director of the Chinese Heritage Church Collaborative. Enoch enjoys spending time with his family, running, martial arts, and playing the occasional video game.

Hanley Liu serves as the English lead pastor at First Chinese Baptist Church of Walnut, California (FCBCW) and serves on the SOLA Network Council. He is happily married to his wife Meryl, and they have two children. He is a graduate of Biola University (BA, 2003), Talbot School of Theology (MDiv, 2006), and the Southern Baptist Theological Seminary (DMin, 2017).

Soojin Park (BA Cornell University; MDiv Reformed Theological Seminary) is the events manager for The Gospel Coalition (TGC). She previously served on staff at Christ Central Presbyterian Church in Centreville, Virginia, as director of youth ministry and adult education. Soojin is a member of the editorial board at SOLA Network and cohost of the *Glo* podcast at TGC.

Jason M. Tarn is the lead English pastor of Houston Chinese Church, a nondenominational Chinese heritage church in Houston, Texas. He received his bachelor's degree from University of Texas at Austin and completed an MDiv at Regent College. Jason grew up at Houston Chinese Church as a teenager and has been pastoring there since 2011. His passion is to bring sound doctrine and missional vision to the immigrant church. He is married to Theresa and has two daughters, Talia and Maisie.

Heidi K. Wong (BS Cornell University; MABS Reformed Theological Seminary) is the executive director for Exilic Church in New York City. Prior to entering vocational ministry, she worked in management consulting and tech. She is a writing fellow for the Washington Institute for Faith, Vocation, and Culture and editor in chief for SOLA Network.

NOTES

Introduction

1. James Emery White, *The Rise of the Nones: Understanding and Reaching the Religiously Unaffiliated* (Grand Rapids: Baker, 2014).

2. Gregory A. Smith, "About Three-in-Ten U.S. Adults Are Now Religiously Unaffiliated," Pew Research Center, December 14, 2021, accessed on December 16, 2023, https://www.pewresearch.org/religion/2021/12/14/about-three-in-ten-u-s-adults-are-now-religiously-unaffiliated/.

3. Jim Davis and Michael Graham, *The Great Dechurching: Who's Leaving, Why Are They Going, and What Will It Take to Bring Them Back?* (Grand Rapids: Zondervan Reflective, 2023), xxii.

4. Timothy Keller, "American Christianity is Due for a Revival," *The Atlantic*, February 5, 2023, accessed on December 15, 2023, https://www.theatlantic.com/ideas/archive/2023/02/christianity-secularization-america-renewal-modernity/672948/.

5. United States Census Bureau, "Quick Facts," *Census.gov*, accessed on December 16, 2023, https://www.census.gov/quickfacts/fact/table/US/PST045222.

6. Jonathan Vespa, Lauren Medina, and David M. Armstrong, "Demographic Turning Points for the United States: Population Projections for 2020 to 2060," issued March 2018, revised February 2020, P25-1144, *Census.gov*, accessed on December 16, 2023, https://www.census.gov/content/dam/Census/library/publications/2020/demo/p25-1144.pdf.

7. Besheer Mohamed and Michael Rotolo, "Religion Among Asian Americans," Pew Research Center, October 11, 2023, accessed on December 16, 2023, https://www.pewresearch.org/religion/2023/10/11/religion-among-asian-americans/.

8. Michael Graham, Steve S. Chang, and Kevin Yi, "Asian American Christians and the Great Dechurching: An Interview with Author Michael Graham," SOLA Network, November 29, 2023, accessed on December 16, 2023, https://sola.network/article/asian-american-christians-and-the-great-dechurching-interview/.

9. Abby Budiman and Neil G. Ruiz, "Key Facts about Asian Americans, a Diverse and Growing Population," Pew Research Center, April 29, 2021, accessed on December 16, 2023, https://www.pewresearch.org/short-reads/2021/04/29/key-facts-about-asian-americans/.

10. Mohamed and Rotolo, "Religion Among Asian Americans."

1 Hidden Beauty
11. Abby Budiman and Neil G. Ruiz, "Key Facts about Asian Americans, a Diverse and Growing Population," Pew Research Center, April 29, 2021, accessed on September 30, 2023, https://www.pewresearch.org/short-reads/2021/04/29/key-facts-about-asian-americans/.

4 Safe Spaces
12. Discovering the Honor-Shame Cultural Paradigm," *Knowledge Workx*, June 18, 2019, updated March 1, 2023, accessed on September 22, 2023, https://www.knowledgeworkx.com/post/discovering-the-honor-shame-cultural-paradigm.
13. Donald A. Russell, "Identifying Character Strengths and Virtue as the Efficacious Component of the Therapist's Person." *Edification: The Transdisciplinary Journal of Christian Psychology* 3, no. 2 (2009), 49.
14. Bruce E. Wampold, *The Great Psychotherapy Debate: Models, Methods, and Findings* (Mahwah, NJ: Lawrence Erlbaum, 2001).
15. J. C. Norcross and B. E. Wampold, "Evidence-Based Therapy Relationships: Research Conclusions and Clinical Practices," *Psychotherapy* 48, no. 1 (2011): 98–102, https://doi.org/10.1037/a0022161; Cristoph Flückiger, A. C. Del Re, B. E. Wampold, and A. O. Horvath, "The Alliance in Adult Psychotherapy: A Meta-Analytic Synthesis," *Psychotherapy (Chic)* 55, no. 4 (2018): 316–340.
16. Daniel Goleman, "What Makes a Leader?," in *On Emotional Intelligence* (Boston: Harvard Business Review Press, 2015), 3.

5 Bridging the Gap
17. Benjamin C. Shin and Sheryl Takagi Silzer, *Tapestry of Grace: Untangling the Cultural Complexities in Asian American Life and Ministry* (Eugene, OR: Wipf & Stock, 2016), 33.

7 Hopeful Exiles
18. J. R. R. Tolkien, *The Fellowship of the Ring* (London: Harper Collins, 1991).
19. John Bunyan, *The Pilgrim's Progress* (Philadelphia: Charles Foster, 1891).
20. G. K. Chesterton, *Orthodoxy* (New York: John Lane, 1908), 147.
21. Eugene Park, "'Minari: Searching for Eden in Arkansas," *The Gospel Coalition*, February 12, 2021, accessed on August 14, 2023, https://www.thegospelcoalition.org/article/minari-searching-for-a-garden/.
22. Esau McCaulley, *Reading While Black: African American Biblical Interpretation as an Exercise in Hope* (Downers Grove, IL: InterVarsity Press, 2020).

23. Ralph Ellison, *Invisible Man* (New York: Random House, 1947).

24. Jay Caspian Kang, *The Loneliest Americans* (New York: Crown, 2021).

25. Jay Caspian Kang, "The Many Lives of Steven Yeun," *New York Times Magazine*, February 3, 2021, accessed on August 14, 2023, https://www.nytimes.com/2021/02/03/magazine/steven-yeun.html.

26. Douglas Martin, "Kosuke Koyama, 79, an Ecumenical Theologian, Dies," *New York Times*, March 31, 2009, accessed on August 14, 2023, https://www.nytimes.com/2009/04/01/world/asia/01koyama.html.

8 Exegete Your People

27. Mia Tuan, *Forever Foreigners or Honorary Whites? The Asian Ethnic Experience Today* (New Brunswick, NJ: Rutgers University Press, 1998), 155.

28. Neil G. Ruiz, Carolyne Im, and Ziyao Tian, "2. Asian Americans and the 'Forever Foreigner' Stereotype," Pew Research Center, accessed on December 22, 2023, https://www.pewresearch.org/race-ethnicity/2023/11/30/asian-americans-and-the-forever-foreigner-stereotype/.

29. Sharon Kim, *A Faith of Our Own: Second-Generation Spirituality in Korean American Churches* (New Brunswick, NJ: Rutgers University Press, 2010), 11.

9 Finding Our Voice

30. Matthew D. Kim and Daniel L. Wong, *Finding Our Voice: A Vision for Asian North American Preaching* (Bellingham, WA: Lexham, 2020).

31. Matthew Richard Sheldon Todd, *English Ministry Crisis in Chinese Canadian Churches: Towards the Retention of English-Speaking Adults from Chinese Canadian Churches through Associated Parallel Independent English Congregation Models* (Eugene, OR: Wipf & Stock, 2015), xiii.

10 Shepherding Singles

32. Richard Fry and Kim Parker, "Rising Share of U.S. Adults Are Living Without a Spouse or Partner," Pew Research, Center, October 5, 2021, accessed on January 1, 2024, https://www.pewresearch.org/social-trends/2021/10/05/rising-share-of-u-s-adults-are-living-without-a-spouse-or-partner/.

12 Heart Matters

33. The discussion here is a very broad look at this topic. Although the primary focus is on East Asian American leaders, even within that group there are too many nuances to address with any detail.

34. For example, there is a difference between an Asian American and someone from a majority culture working in the same predominantly Asian American church (even though the context is the same), because of what goes on in our hearts.

35. Because of space constraints, this chapter will focus on only the negative impact of the Asian American culture on our hearts. However, this does not negate the many beautiful and blessed aspects of the culture that have the potential to bring God great glory.

36. We could consider many ideas when looking into what influences the hearts of Asian Americans (honor/shame, fear of man, status as minorities, maintaining harmony, respecting authority, etc.), but because of the large range of how those ideas affect people (even within the different Asian cultures), I chose to focus on one idea.

37. This was then often perpetuated and deepened by the church culture. The kids who were extolled were those who succeeded in some way, that is, they got into the prestigious university, excelled in in music, or generally reflected well on their family.

38. By this I don't mean it is the only motive, but it is often there lurking in the recesses of our hearts.

39. We will consider these three ideas, but they are representative of so many of our responses (e.g., discouragement, frustration, impatience, hopelessness, depression, confusion).

40. For example, prayer, repentance, meditation, replacing lies with truth, considering the reap and sow principle, and so forth.

41. C. H. Spurgeon, *Morning and Evening: Daily Readings* (Albany, OR: SAGE Software, 1996), November 11 PM, 635, accessed on January 1, 2024, https://www.monergism.com/thethreshold/sdg/spurgeon/CHS_Morning_and_Evening_Daily_Readings.PDF.

13 Silencing Shame

42. Ken Shigematsu, *Now I Become Myself: How Deep Grace Heals Our Shame and Restores Our True Self* (Grand Rapids: Zondervan, 2023), 1.

43. Bryan Robinson, "10 Signs You Could Be Working Yourself to Death In a Hybrid World," *Forbes*, October 7, 2022, accessed on December 16, 2023, https://www.forbes.com/sites/bryanrobinson/2022/10/07/10-signs-you-could-be-working-yourself-to-death-in-a-hybrid-world/?sh=6b08c8b92e29.

44. Brené Brown, *Daring Greatly: How the Courage to Be Vulnerable Transforms the*

Way We Live, Love, Parent, and Lead (New York: Gothom, 2012).

15 Steadfast

45. *Beef*, episode 8, "The Drama of Original Choice," directed by Lee Sung Kin, written by Lee Sung Jin and Jean Kyoung Frazier, aired April 6, 2023, on Netflix, 9:35.

46. "Excerpt: A Rapid Decline in Pastoral Security," *Barna*, March 15, 2023, accessed on September 29, 2023, https://www.barna.com/research/pastoral-security-confidence/.

47. Benjamin C. Shin and Sheryl Takagi Silzer, *Tapestry of Grace: Untangling the Cultural Complexities in Asian American Life and Ministry* (Eugene, OR: Wipf & Stock, 2016), 33.

48. Jayson Georges, *The 3D Gospel: Ministry in Guilt, Shame, and Fear Cultures* (Timē Press, 2014), Kindle ed., 20.

49. Peter Cha, S. Steve Kang, and Helen Lee, eds., *Growing Healthy Asian American Churches* (Downers Grove, IL: 2006), 61.

50. *Church Answers* (blog); "The Life Cycle of a Pastor," by Thom Rainer, posted on April 24, 2023, accessed on September 29, 2023, https://churchanswers.com/blog/the-life-cycle-of-a-pastor-updated/.

51. Kye S. Chung, Panel Discussion on Pastoral Leadership at the 4th EM Pastors Conference, Princeton Seminary, April 13, 2010.

52. Eugene H. Peterson, *A Long Obedience in the Same Direction: Discipleship in an Instant Society* (Downers Grove, IL: InterVarsity Press, 1980).

SOLA Network exists to influence the emerging generation of Asian Americans and those who lead them with the Gospel of Jesus Christ. Find our articles, book reviews, podcasts, and more at **SOLA.NETWORK**. If you would like to partner with SOLA Network through collaboration, networking, volunteering, or giving, please contact us through our website.

Made in the USA
Middletown, DE
20 April 2024

53234530R00116